OPERA
A New Way of Listening

Author's acknowledgments
I am most grateful to Rachel Aris, Clare Shedden and
the dedicated team at De Agostini Editions; to Caroline
Dawnay at Peters, Fraser and Dunlop; and to family
and friends for their invaluable advice and support.

First published
by De Agostini Editions
Interpark House
7 Down Street
London W1Y 7DS

Distributed in the U.S.
by Stewart, Tabori & Chang,
a division of US Media Holdings Inc
575 Broadway
New York NY 10012

Distributed in Canada
by General Publishing Company Ltd
30 Lesmill Road, Don Mills
Ontario M3B 2T6

A CIP catalogue record for this book is available from
the British Library.

Library of Congress Cataloging-in-Publication Data

Waugh, Alexander
         Opera : a new way of listening / Alexander Waugh.
                  p. cm.
         Includes index.
         ISBN 1-899883-72-X
         1. Operas—Analysis, appreciation.   I. Title
MT95.W33   1996
782.1—dc20   96-23051
                                              CIP
                                              MN

Publishing Director Frances Gertler
Art Director Tim Foster
Senior Editor Rachel Aris
Senior Art Editor Clare Shedden
Editorial Assistants Philippa Cooper, Becky Lister
Picture Researcher Julia Ruxton

UK ISBN 1 899883 71 1
US ISBN 1 899883 72 X

Printed in Italy
by Officine Grafiche De Agostini, Novara
Bound by Legatoria del Verbano S.p.A

OPERA
A New Way
of Listening

Alexander Waugh

De Agostini *Editions*

CONTENTS

CD RUNNING ORDER

1 Massenet: "Nicias! Ah" from *Thaïs*, Act II (extract)
2 Puccini: "Se la giurata" from *Tosca*, Act II (extract)
3 Donizetti: mad scene from *Lucia di Lammermoor*, Act III (extract)
4 Mozart: overture from *Don Giovanni* (extract)
5 Wagner: overture from *Die Meistersinger von Nürnberg* (extract)
6 Monteverdi: overture from *L'Orfeo* (extract)
7 Verdi: overture from *Aida* (extract)
8 Puccini: overture from *La Bohème* (extract)
9 Handel: "Ah! Ruggiero crudel" from *Alcina*, Act II (extract)
10 Beethoven: "Abscheulicher!" from *Fidelio*, Act I (extract)
11 Wagner: "Was Macht dich" from *Lohengrin*, Act II (extract)
12 Wagner: "Schläfst du" from *Götterdämmerung*, Act II (extracts)
13 Verdi: "Celeste Aida" from *Aida*, Act I (extracts)
14 Verdi: "O patria mia" from *Aida*, Act III (extracts)
15 Mozart: "Der Hölle Rache" from *Die Zauberflöte*, Act II (extract)
16 Verdi: "L'abborita rivale" from *Aida*, Act IV (extract)
17 Sullivan: "Alone and yet alive" from *The Mikado*, Act II (extract)
18 Handel: "Ombra mai fu" from *Serse*, Act I (extract)
19 Wagner: "Wie sie selig" from *Tristan und Isolde*, Act III (extract)
20 Mozart: "Non più andrai" from *Le nozze di Figaro*, Act I (extract)
21 Donizetti: "Ah! Un foco insolito" from *Don Pasquale*, Act I (extract)
22 Verdi: "Il santo nome" from *La forza del destino*, Act II (extract)
23 Verdi: "Va pensiero" from *Nabucco*, Act III (extract)
24 Monteverdi: "Vi ricorda" from *L'Orfeo*, Act II (extract)
25 Gluck: "Che farò senza Euridice?" from *Orfeo ed Euridice*, Act III (extract)
26 Bellini: "Casta diva" from *Norma*, Act I (extract)
27 Puccini: "Quando me'n vo' soletta" from *La Bohème*, Act II (extract)
28 Purcell: "When I am laid in earth" from *Dido and Aeneas*, Act III
29 Purcell: overture from *Dido and Aeneas*, Act I
30 Mozart: "Là ci darem la mano" from *Don Giovanni*, Act I
31 Mozart: "Madamina il catalogo" from *Don Giovanni*, Act I (extract)
32 Rossini: "Largo al factotum" from *Il barbiere di Siviglia*, Act I
33 Rossini: Overture from *Il barbiere di Siviglia* (extract)
34 Verdi: "Bella figlia dell'amore" from *Rigoletto*, Act III
35 Verdi: "La donna è mobile" from *Rigoletto*, Act III
36 Wagner: "Morgenlich leuchtend" from *Die Meistersinger von Nürnberg*, Act III
37 Wagner: Riot scene from *Die Meistersinger von Nürnberg*, Act II (extract)
38 Mussorgsky: Coronation scene from *Boris Godunov*, Act I
39 Mussorgsky: Finale from *Boris Godunov*, Act IV (extract)
40 Bizet: "L'amour est un oiseau rebelle" (Habanera) from *Carmen*, Act I
41 Bizet: Death scene from *Carmen*, Act IV (extract)
42 Puccini: "Vissi d'arte" from *Tosca*, Act II
43 Puccini: "Recondita armonia" from *Tosca*, Act I (extract)

INTRODUCTION

Opera is more popular now than it has ever been in its four-hundred-year history. It has become a global phenomenon, enjoyed by people of all kinds and all cultures. With this boom has come a need for a greater understanding of opera – for opera, like any other art form, is best enjoyed when it is properly understood.

Opera: A New Way of Listening provides all the basic tools you need to enjoy any opera. With the help of dozens of musical extracts on the accompanying CD, the book explains all the different categories of voice and how to recognize them, gives plot outlines for over 100 of the world's best-loved operas and discusses how to prepare for a trip to the opera. The heart of the book explores how to get the most from opera by looking in detail at the eight of the world's greatest operas. A pivotal song from each of these is featured on the CD and decoded on an annotated "time-line," which charts moment by moment what is happening musically and dramatically and explores the many ways a composer can bring a librettist's text to life.

But understanding opera is not simply about grasping the twists and turns of the plot or knowing how to respond to the music: there is so much more that goes into making an opera work that we might not at first perceive. So this book also looks at opera from the point of view of the performers, directors and technicians responsible for putting an opera on the stage. By providing insights into every aspect of opera, it is hoped that this book will make any trip to the opera a truly enjoyable experience for the newcomer and confirmed enthusiast alike.

CHAPTER ONE

The Opera Experience

*One of the most magnificent and expenseful diversions the wit
of man can invent.*
English diarist, John Evelyn, writing of opera in 1645

Opposite Calaf, played by Placido
Domingo, prepares to die for his love
of the icy princess, Turandot, who gave
her name to Puccini's last opera.

Opera is a unique and lavish art form quite unlike any other. It
cannot be compared to film, theatre, ballet or music at a concert.
Opera has its own life force, and when its many disparate elements –
solos, ensembles, choruses, lighting, design, orchestra, movement and
dance – work together, it can be one of the most exhilarating and
captivating of all the performing arts. But in order to enjoy an opera
we first need to understand exactly what it is that we are looking at
and listening to. We need to exorcise any misconceptions we might have
about it, to accept that opera is not a play with music or even a concert
with a play appended to it, but a vital art form that exists in its own
right. Armed with this information we can truly relish any opera.

In many ways opera is the easiest of all the musical arts to appreciate because it consists of a three-way process between the words, the
music and the visual presentation, each helping to explain the other.
The words and the drama, for instance, tell us what the music is
supposed to mean. In other words, if a character on stage is saying "I
feel so depressed that I want to kill myself," then we can assume that
the music accompanying this morbid sentiment might be intended to
reflect or even amplify the same moods and emotions as the words. We
get no such help listening to a string quartet, a sonata or a symphony.

Showing emotion. *Top* Luciano Pavarotti in the comic role of Nemorino in Donizetti's *L'elisir d'amore*. *Above* A despairing José Carreras with Teresa Berganza in the last tragic scene of Bizet's *Carmen*.

With pure music it is up to the listener to decide what the sound is supposed to mean.

Just as the words of an opera are able to bring meaning to the music, so the music also enhances the meaning of the words. For example, if a character is angry, the music he or she is singing will be loud, erratic and disturbed – imitating the voice and actions of an angry person (**CD track 1**). If a heroine is hysterical her voice will swoop and shriek (**CD track 2**), imitating and exaggerating real life. Madness, another common operatic theme, is often portrayed with music that is disjointed or confused (**CD track 3**). Sobs and tears can also be made to sound pitifully realistic; so can laughter or pain. There is no end to the inventiveness with which composers have managed to match their music to the extremes and subtleties of human emotion, and that is ultimately the strength of opera. So in opera, as in more abstract music (that is, music without words), the movement of the music is used to awaken the senses of the listeners and arouse their emotions through its extraordinary power of suggestion. Music can even be used to such subtle effect as to tell the audience that the words sung by a character are hiding his true feelings. Wagner, for example, used a complex system of leitmotifs in some of his operas. Leitmotifs are themes to which the composer has ascribed a specific meaning. Using this system a composer could write a tune and label it "Lying," so that every time the tune is sung or played by the orchestra the audience might assume that somebody on stage is not telling the truth.

So if opera is such an easy art form to enjoy, why should anyone need a book to explain how to enjoy it? The simple reason is that opera is a vast subject – the repertoire of operas spans four centuries and many languages – so it is helpful to be pointed in the right direction. Opera is also a very artificial art form, in the sense that most of what is said and happens in opera is unlikely ever to occur in real life. What is more, it is an extremely expensive entertainment to mount. These factors have led to a whole host of misconceptions that have done little to help or encourage newcomers into opera. It may be useful, therefore, to clarify the following points:

What is an opera?

Opera is a sung stage drama set (usually) to continuous music.

What is special about opera as an art form?

The combination of music and words is capable, at its most sublime, of telling us things about human character, feeling, mood and motivation that music or words on their own are powerless to express.

What is special about opera as an entertainment?

Opera is the most exciting, the most involving and often the most spectacular of all the performing arts, combining all the great skills of song, instrumental playing, drama, dance and design into one.

The components of an opera

More than any form of music, opera is an Event. It brings together many of the arts.
Harold C. Schonberg, *The New York Times*

In order to enjoy an opera thoroughly, it is essential that you understand the form of what you are about to experience before arriving at the opera house or listening to a recording. Of course, no two operas are identical but many of them share the same basic structure. Most begin with an overture: a short orchestral piece that settles the audience and prepares the listeners for the atmosphere of the drama to come. Sometimes the overture contains musical themes that will later reappear

The lavish set for Act I of this Veronese production of Puccini's *Tosca* is an extravagant representation of the church of Saint Andrea della Valle in Rome.

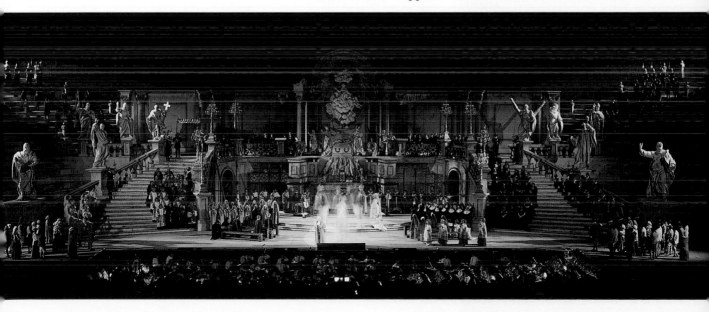

in the main part of the opera. Mozart's overture to *Don Giovanni*, for example, incorporates music that is used again in the dramatic denouement of the final scene (**CD track 4**); so too does Wagner's overture to *Die Meistersinger von Nürnberg* (The Meistersingers of Nuremberg), which introduces the melody of Walther's prize-winning song halfway through (*see pages 86–93*, **CD tracks 5** and **36**). The music on **CD tracks 6** to **8** demonstrates a range of operatic openings by Monteverdi, Verdi and Puccini. The overtures to Gilbert and Sullivan's

The Korean soprano Sumi Jo playing the Queen of the Night from Mozart's *Die Zauberflöte* (The Magic Flute), which she has made one of her speciality roles. The Queen's vengeful second aria with its incredibly high notes is the opera's most virtuosic moment. Edita Gruberová can be heard singing an extract from this aria on track 15 of the CD.

comic operettas are simply medleys of all the best tunes. In many instances, though, overtures consist of music that will not be heard again. In certain operas where the music is less self-contained and more atmospheric, the term "prelude" is often used instead of "overture."

Most operas are divided, just like plays, into acts. Five acts are common, especially for French and Russian "grand opera" (*see page 48*), but comic operas more usually consist of one or two acts. Tragedies may comprise any number of acts. Each act is generally made up of arias (solo songs), ensembles (duets, trios, quartets and so on) and choruses linked by what is known as recitative – a form of sung dialogue that, in pitch and rhythm, is more closely related to dramatic speech than to song. So, while arias are used to express the poetic concerns of the principal characters (such as sadness, happiness, loss or triumph) and serve as the emotional focus of each act, recitatives are used to fill in the details of speech and plot in a sort of musical prose.

Be prepared

Whenever I go to the opera, I leave my sense and reason at the door with my half-guinea and deliver myself up to my eyes and my ears.
Lord Chesterfield in a letter to his son, 23 January 1752

Even the most trenchant and well-informed opera buff needs to prepare before going out to the opera – and that doesn't mean brushing your hair and putting on smart clothes! Preparing means, at the very least, reading a synopsis of the plot before the curtain goes up. You will get so much more from an opera if you know who is who and what is going on. Even if the opera is being performed in your mother tongue it is never possible to hear absolutely all the words. The more thorough the preparation, the more you will enjoy the opera – it is as simple as that. Some might find the suggestions listed *right* excessive, but when you consider how expensive most opera tickets are and what a treat it is to visit the opera house, then following these pointers is well worth the effort.

A willing suspension of disbelief

No good opera plot can be sensible, for people do not sing when they are feeling sensible.
W.H. Auden, 1961

Opera has never been famous for the coherence or logic of its plots, and for those who consider themselves "plot sensitive," some of opera's stories can seem too ridiculous for words. Samuel Johnson's famous dictionary defines opera as "an exotic and irrational entertainment." This was written in the eighteenth century, but no one could really argue that opera has become obviously more rational since then. For instance, did Wagner really expect his audience to believe in the central love affair in his *Der fliegende Holländer* (The Flying Dutchman) between the daughter of a Norwegian sailor and an accursed ghost of a flying Dutchman? And how are we to accept that the two lovers from Verdi's *La forza del destino*, Alvaro and Leonora, should be reunited following years of separation after Alvaro has enrolled as a monk and Leonora has chosen to become a hermit coincidentally along the road from Alvaro's monastery?

PREPARING FOR THE OPERA

1 Read a synopsis of the plot. Many opera dictionaries contain synopses, but if you cannot get hold of one, arrive early: there is always a synopsis in the programme.

2 Read up on the history of the opera and find out when the important arias and other key moments occur.

3 Listen to a complete recording of the opera if possible, or at least try to hear a recording of the highlights.

4 Read the libretto (the words of the opera). Most CD booklets feature the libretto and translation, and since so many operas are sung in a foreign language it is well worth reading and understanding the text beforehand. This doesn't take long. The complete text of Puccini's *La Bohème*, for instance, can be read in under twenty minutes.

5 Where the opera is based on a famous book, try to read the original. If it is based on a true historical figure or event, find out the real facts. This isn't always possible, but where it is, it very much helps you to develop a profounder understanding of the opera and its setting.

Many operas have rather unlikely plots. The main character in Janáček's *The Makropulos Affair* (**left**, played by Anja Silja), for example, is supposed to be 337 years old, while Fiordiligi and Dorabella in Mozart's *Così fan tutte* (**right**) fail to recognize their fiancés even though they are only thinly disguised as Albanians.

Madness is an emotion that works well in opera. **Above** The enraged, lovestruck Orlando (Marilyn Horne) threatens Angelica (soprano Ruth Ann Swenson), frustrated that she will not return his love in a production of Handel's *Orlando* at San Francisco Opera. For this scene, Handel composed music with five beats to the bar – the only time he used this musical form. **Above right** Philip Langridge as fisherman Peter Grimes in Benjamin Britten's opera. Grimes is sent mad by the desperate and lonely circumstances of his life.

In opera anything can happen and this is something we must accept. Heroines can and do die for no apparent medical reason; they simply collapse from a heady blend of sorrow and frustration. Madness is also a central theme of many operas, from Handel's *Orlando* (whose famous mad scene includes some of the most unusual music Handel ever wrote) to Donizetti's famous *Lucia di Lammermoor*, Bellini's *I Puritani*, Stravinsky's *The Rake's Progress* and Benjamin Britten's *Peter Grimes*. Characters in opera may also say far sillier things than they do in real life – or perhaps it is that the grandeur of the operatic form can sometimes seem out of step with the need to convey everyday information. Here is an extract from the libretto of Schubert's *Alfonso und Estrella* (1822):

Chorus: The princess has appeared.

King: The princess?

Chorus: The princess.

King: Has she appeared? Has she appeared?

Chorus: Yes, she has appeared, she is approaching the palace.

King: She is coming here.

Chorus: She is approaching the palace, she is coming here.

King: Bitter grief depart, joy shines again. Where can she be so long?

Chorus: I see her hurrying. I see her hurrying.

King: Where can she be so long?...

Chorus: She is near now.

This is probably a cruel example to drag out – Schubert's opera was never a roaring success even in its own day – but so many operas, including some of the most popular and enduring works, are full of exchanges as banal and unlikely as this.

The American radio comedian, Ed Gardner, once said that: "opera is when a guy gets stabbed in the back and, instead of bleeding, he sings." In real life people don't sing at each other, so we might argue that the whole premise on which opera is based is completely pointless. But art, in any form, has rarely been about realism. The fantasy and make-believe in opera should be treated as an integral part of the experience and one of the main reasons why opera is such an enjoyable form of entertainment.

Another myth that needs to be dispelled right away is that opera singers have to be fat to be good at their job. True, some well-known opera singers are considerably overweight, but no correlation between obesity and ability to sing has ever been proved. Wagner was so embarrassed by the size of Ludwig Schnorr, the tenor appointed to sing in the premiere of *Tristan und Isolde*, that the composer had to consider removing him from the production altogether for fear of ridicule. In the event nobody else could sing the part so he was stuck with Schnorr and his large wife, Malvina, in the title roles. Sometimes opera singers are undeniably too fat for the roles they are supposed to be portraying. Slowly fashions are changing and perhaps there is now more of an onus on singers to attend to their appearance than there has been for the last hundred years. But whatever the stage appearance of our hero and heroine we must suspend our thirst for reality or, as the great Tchaikovsky so aptly put it: "I have never encountered anything more false and foolish than the effort to get truth into opera. In opera everything is based upon the not-true."

Words and music: an ideal partnership?

Count: Opera is an absurdity. Orders are delivered in song, politics discussed in a duet…and dagger blows are dealt in melody.

Clairon: I could get used to people dying with an aria, but why are the words always worse than the music? Why must they owe their power of expression to it?

From the libretto to Richard Strauss's opera, *Capriccio* (1942), by Clemens Krauss

An unlikely pose for a real conversation: Bryn Terfel and Thomas Hampson face the audience to talk to each other in this production of *Don Giovanni* at the Metropolitan Opera House, New York.

Kiri Te Kanawa as Countess Madeleine in Richard Strauss's last opera *Capriccio*. The whole libretto is an intellectual debate about the relative importance of words and music in opera.

Are the words or the music more important in an opera? This is a question that always vexes everybody. Mozart said that "in opera the text must be the obedient daughter of the music." His great contemporary, Gluck, took very much the opposite line: "I have thought it necessary to reduce music to its true function," he wrote, "which is that of seconding poetry in the expression of sentiments and dramatic situations of a story, neither interrupting the action nor detracting from its vividness by useless and superfluous ornament."

Perhaps the finer points of this issue can be left to the music theorists and aestheticians, but there is no doubt that a basic understanding of the whole question of words and music is a great help in appreciating why opera is like it is. "Why," people often ask, "do operas have to be so long? And why are the stories often so illogical and little thought through?" Often the answers lie in the simple battle between the words and the music.

When a composer and a librettist sit down to write an opera they have to think to themselves: what is opera best at? What are its strengths and what are its limitations? Obviously there are certain things that music cannot express and words can. "Please could you pass the salt," for instance, is a sentiment that music could not enunciate purely on its own. Similarly there are moods and feelings aroused by music that words alone could only gropingly convey. Because opera is a music-based art form, large portions of each act (which in a theatrical play might be given over to the development of plot or other finer details) have to be reserved for scenes of mood and feeling. That is why, in opera, the story lines are often so thin. Operas are concerned not with plots but with states of mind.

The solution for early composers, especially in the eighteenth century, was to include recitative which, as we have seen, is bland music devised so that a character can impart essential information without the encumbrance of more heavily emotive music that would distract attention from the words. Often accompanied only by simple chords on the harpsichord, it is particularly prominent in the operas of Handel, Mozart and Rossini. The examples of accompanied recitative on **CD tracks 9–11** show how Handel, Beethoven and Wagner each imitated the effect of dramatic speech. In some parts of Beethoven's *Fidelio* and Bizet's *Carmen*, spoken dialogue is used instead of recitative. The French playwright Pierre Augustin de Beaumarchais (whose farces formed the basis for Mozart's *Le nozze di Figaro* and Rossini's *Il barbiere di Siviglia*), neatly summed up the whole issue of words and music in his preface to *Tarare*: "Music is in the opera what the verses are in the drama – a more stately expression, a stronger means of presenting thoughts and emotions."

Elitism and opera snobbery

If opera lovers are so enamoured of such arcane boring stuff, let them pay more for their tickets. In any case, many of these stuffed shirts go to the opera only as a social occasion to fraternise with their equally over-privileged friends.
From a reader's letter to London's *Evening Standard* newspaper, 5 July 1995

Opera has been dogged by accusations of snobbery and elitism from its appearance early in the seventeenth century right up until the present day. To begin with, opera was paid for by a ruler and performed in front of an invited audience of friends and courtiers at his palace. Later, when opera moved into opera houses, the aristocrats and wealthy merchants occupying the Grand Tier boxes were largely responsible for the financial success of the opera house. The conventional horse-shoe shape of the opera house was originally

Opera needn't be an elitist art: crowds at Covent Garden market in London watch as Placido Domingo is relayed live from the opera house to a giant screen outside (**above** and **right**). **Above right** Opera-lovers queue to watch the performance.

17

designed not just to limit the distance between the stage and the furthest point in the auditorium but also to display an affluent audience of box-holders to each other.

Opera is such an expensive entertainment to stage (and needs to be performed in such a small space, relatively speaking) that good tickets will always be expensive. Sales of tickets have never been able to cover the costs of soloists, chorus, orchestra, sets, designers, lighting, rehearsals, administration and all the other myriad costs entailed in putting on an opera, so opera needs patronage of one sort or another – either, as in the past, from the wealthy aristocracy or, as now, from state funding and business sponsorship. The expense of the tickets does not mean that opera is an elitist entertainment, however. Holidays are expensive, after all, as well as any number of other pleasures. It is all a question of priorities. Indeed, opera today is enjoyed by more people and a far bigger cross-section of society than at any other time in its history. What really matters now is not who is in the auditorium but what is happening on the stage.

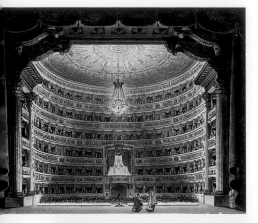

The question of language

I do not mind what language an opera is sung in so long as it is a language I don't understand.
Nobel prize-winning physicist, Sir Edward Appleton, 1955

Should an opera be translated into the language of the people who are watching, or is it always better to hear an opera in the language in which it was originally written? Well, the question is a thorny one – many people still think it odd that opera should be so enjoyed in foreign languages. As long ago as 1710, the English essayist Joseph Addison wrote that "our grandchildren will be curious to know the reason why their forefathers used to sit together like an audience of foreigners in their own country, and to hear whole plays acted before them in a tongue which they did not understand."

Top Inside the Scala Opera House at Milan. The traditional layout of a grand opera house ensured that people of social prominence had the best seats. Boxes from the second row up were for the aristocrats while the ground floor was originally intended for major-domos, secretaries and other senior servants of the nobility. **Above** At the outdoor arena in Verona a vast audience watches an opera. The spectacle is grand but some of the intimacy of the smaller opera houses is inevitably lost.

The problem of language has been partially resolved in the bigger opera houses today by the introduction of surtitles, whereby a simultaneous translation of the words is projected on to a screen just above the stage. An innovative alternative is offered at the Metropolitan Opera House in New York where the translated text is fed into small monitors, placed in front of every seat, that can be switched on or off at will. Obviously the sound of the words is crucial to composers when they are setting a text to music and it is therefore preferable, wherever possible, to hear an opera in the original language – even if it is a language you do not understand. The two extracts on **CD Track 12** demonstrate how different an aria (a short solo from Wagner's *Götterdämmerung*) can sound depending on the language in which it is sung. You will notice how the whole timbre and type of sound is completely different in English. Composers are primarily concerned with sound and if the sound can be changed as radically as this just by translating the words, then the conclusion to be drawn must be that translating opera is not necessarily a good thing. Indeed, to some people, translating the language is as sacrilegious as changing the instrumentation in the orchestra or singing the whole song in a completely different key. Remember that even when an opera is sung in your own mother tongue it is never possible to catch all the words. If you have a choice, try to hear an opera in its original language, especially when surtitle translations are provided – but, whatever language the opera is in, you will still benefit from preparing thoroughly before you go.

Below A performance of the second opera of Wagner's Ring, *Die Walküre*, at the San Francisco Opera House, where English surtitles are screened above the stage. *Bottom* Scenes of the hedonistic kingdom of Venusberg in this production of Wagner's *Tannhäuser* at Vienna State Opera provide an entertaining spectacle even for those who cannot speak German.

CHAPTER TWO
The Elements of Opera

Producing an opera for the stage – or even making a recording – requires a huge diversity of talent, not all of it musical. From sound and lighting engineers to prompters and administrative staff, there is often an army of hundreds at work behind the scenes, all contributing to the success of an opera. Chapter Three will take a look backstage at an opera house. This chapter, however, examines the most visible elements of opera: the soloists, chorus, director, conductor, orchestra and ballet.

The singers

The singers are the stars of the opera and always have been. In the eighteenth century the great castrati (*see page 24*) such as Senesino and Farinelli earned vast fortunes and were famous all over Europe. The same is true of many singers today, particularly the preeminent tenors and diva sopranos, many of whom have achieved a near godlike status in the eyes and ears of their adoring fans. The best singers have the power to make a production work, almost single handedly, but above all they are able to bring operatic characters to life, to breathe human realism into this most unreal art form.

Singers need to be able to act as well as to sing, but there are some notable exceptions. Luciano Pavarotti, for instance, is not famed for his acting abilities, but his unique voice and distinctive physique give him

Left The elements of opera at work together in a scene from Puccini's *La Bohème* at Verona.

an almost hypnotic presence on stage. The reverse is probably true of the American-Greek soprano Maria Callas, who many consider the greatest diva that ever lived. In fact, her voice, intonation and technical abilities were not always of the highest standard, particularly towards the end of her life, but for those lucky enough to see her perform on stage she was a commanding actress and an extraordinary personality.

In vocal terms, great singers have a rare ability to sound spontaneous. Like actors, singers need to persuade their audience that they are real characters on stage (not just puppets churning out memorized lines), and it is their job to ensure that their gestures, facial expressions and the music they sing are as natural and convincing as possible.

What makes opera so consuming a passion for its fans is the thrill of seeing different singers in the same roles. No two Don Giovannis or Toscas are ever alike and each singer, with his or her own musical and dramatic interpretation of a role, is capable of making even the most

frequently performed opera seem like a new work. Singers are often recognizable vocally by the tone, accent and inflection they use on certain words. Maria Callas, for example, had a strong singing tone, a slight harshness in the middle range of her voice and a thinness on sustained high notes (listen to **CD track 42**). Pavarotti, Domingo and Carreras also have distinctive voices that, with a little practice, are as easy to tell apart as the voices of famous film stars. **CD track 13** features an extract from the aria "Celeste Aida" from Verdi's opera *Aida*, sung in turn by two great tenors: Franco Corelli and Placido Domingo. Listen to the pace, tone and intensity of the two performances, comparing the different approach each singer

It is generally accepted that higher voices sound more dramatic than lower ones, so the heroes and heroines of opera tend to be tenors and sopranos. **Below** Sopranos Angela Gheorghiu (top) and Jessye Norman. **Right** Tenors José Carreras (top) and Placido Domingo.

has taken to his role. Corelli sounds rough, but this and the unevenness of his tone bring raw intensity to his role. Domingo is much sweeter in tone, but his controlled sound is no less passionate. Now listen

VOICE	CD TRACK	KEY ROLES	FAMOUS SINGERS
■ Soprano	15 Mozart: *Die Zauberflöte* Queen of the Night: "Der Hölle Rache" sung by Edita Gruberová	Aida, Butterfly, Isolde, Jenůfa, Lucia di Lammermoor, Mélisande, Norma, Susanna (*Le nozze di Figaro*), Tosca, Violetta (*La traviata*)	Victoria de los Angeles, Montserrat Caballé, Maria Callas, Mirella Freni, Kiri Te Kanawa, Jessye Norman, Joan Sutherland
■ Mezzo-soprano	16 Verdi: *Aida* Amneris: "L'abborita rivale" sung by Fiorenza Cossotto	Amneris (*Aida*), Azucena (*Il trovatore*), Carmen, Maddalena (*Rigoletto*), Rosina (*Il barbiere di Siviglia*)	Janet Baker, Agnes Baltsa, Cecilia Bartoli, Teresa Berganza, Maria Ewing, Marilyn Horne
■ Contralto	17 Sullivan: *The Mikado* Katisha: "Alone and yet alive" sung by Monica Sinclair	Brangäne (*Tristan und Isolde*), Erda and Fricka (*The Ring*), Klytämnestra (*Elektra*), Lucretia (*The Rape of Lucretia*)	Kathleen Ferrier, Ernestine Schumann-Heink, Monica Sinclair, Claramae Turner
■ Alto or counter-tenor	18 Handel: *Serse* "Ombra mai fu" sung by Gérard Lesne	Akhnaten, Giulio Cesare, Oberon (*A Midsummer Night's Dream*), Orfeo (*Orfeo ed Euridice*), Orlando	James Bowman, Michael Chance, Alfred Deller, Jochen Kowalski, Gérard Lesne, Drew Minter
■ Tenor	19 Wagner: *Tristan und Isolde* Tristan: "Wie sie selig" sung by Jon Vickers	Aeneas (*Les Troyens*), Calaf (*Turandot*), Mario Cavaradossi (*Tosca*), Don Carlos, Nemorino (*L'elisir d'amore*), Otello, Peter Grimes, Samson, Siegfried, Walther (*Die Meistersinger von Nürnberg*)	Roberto Alagna, Francisco Araiza, Jussi Björling, José Carreras, Enrico Caruso, José Cura, Placido Domingo, Beniamino Gigli, Siegfried Jerusalem, Luciano Pavarotti
■ Baritone	20 Mozart: *Le nozze di Figaro* Figaro: "Non più Andrai" sung by Giuseppe Taddei	Billy Budd, Escamillo, Figaro, Don Giovanni, Eugene Onegin, Rigoletto, Wozzeck	Thomas Allen, Dietrich Fischer-Dieskau, Tito Gobbi, Dmitri Hvorostovsky
■ Bass-baritone	21 Donizetti: *Don Pasquale* Pasquale: "Ah! Un foco insolito" sung by Sesto Bruscantini	Duke Bluebeard, Baron Ochs (*Der Rosenkavalier*), Hans Sachs (*Die Meistersinger*), Wotan (*The Ring*)	Robert Hale, Benjamin Luxon, Samuel Ramey, John Tomlinson, José van Dam
■ Bass	22 Verdi: *La forza del destino* Padre Guardiano: "Il santo nome" sung by Paul Plishka	Arkel (*Pélleas et Mélisande*), Boris Godunov, Méphistofélès (*Faust*), Philip II (*Don Carlos*)	Owen Brannigan, Fyodor Chaliapin, Boris Christoff, Nicolai Ghiaurov, Ezio Pinza

to CD track 14, which features another aria from the same opera ("O patria mia"), this time sung in turn by the sopranos Birgit Nilsson and Montserrat Caballé. Again, you will hear the clear differences in voice and personality of the two singers.

The four main kinds of operatic voice are soprano and contralto (the highest and lowest female voices), and tenor and bass (high and low male voices). Tenors and sopranos usually have the leading roles, while contraltos and basses take supporting roles; basses often play villainous characters. The other voices you will hear are the mezzo-soprano, which lies between the registers of soprano and contralto, and the baritone, which is between the tenor and bass. There is also a bass-baritone, which is slightly lower and heavier in tone than a baritone. The highest modern adult male voice is the countertenor. In Handel's day, the principal male lead role would have been taken by a castrato, a male singer castrated in boyhood to stop his voice from breaking. As the practice of castrating boy singers died out during the last century, however, the operatic roles created for them were usually taken by a female mezzo-soprano. Nowadays roles such as Gluck's *Orfeo* and Handel's *Giulio Cesare* are generally sung by a male countertenor singing falsetto (that is, in the highest, unbroken range of his voice). Examples of all the eight major types of voice can be heard on **CD** **tracks 15–22** (*see box on page 23*).

Even within the categories of soprano, contralto, tenor and bass there are countless subdivisions. Some basses, for instance, specialize in portentous, grave roles while so-called *buffo* basses are more suited to comic roles. In the tenor register there is a beguiling number of classifications. The *heldentenor* (heroic tenor) has a powerful, enduring sound suitable for the great works of Wagner or Strauss; the dramatic tenor is similarly endowed but is more often associated with Italian and French opera. The lyric tenor, by contrast, is sweeter and quieter in tone and admirably suited to the lighter

The title role of Verdi's last opera, *Falstaff*, is one of many written not for a tenor but for a baritone. In this scene from Act II of the opera, Falstaff is played by Benjamin Luxon and Mistress Quickly by Anne Collins.

repertory. Apart from these there are the *tenor altino* (a very high tenor), the *tenore di forza* (tenor of force), *tenore di grazia* (graceful tenor), *tenore robusto* (robust tenor) and even a *tenore spinto* (pushed tenor), which implies a brilliant if forced tone. There is a similar number of different types of soprano and contralto voice as well.

Not all title roles are taken by the soprano and tenor. Mussorgsky's Boris Godunov is a bass, and many title roles have been written for baritones (Don Giovanni, Figaro in *Il barbiere di Siviglia*, Billy Budd, Wozzeck, Falstaff and Eugene Onegin) and mezzo-sopranos (Carmen, Isabella in *L'Italiana in Algeri* and Angiolina in *La Cenerentola*).

The chorus

The chorus is most often used for crowd scenes and to provide a rousing finale to each act. This can sometimes mean that the drama suffers as huge crowds assemble on stage. At its best, though, the chorus

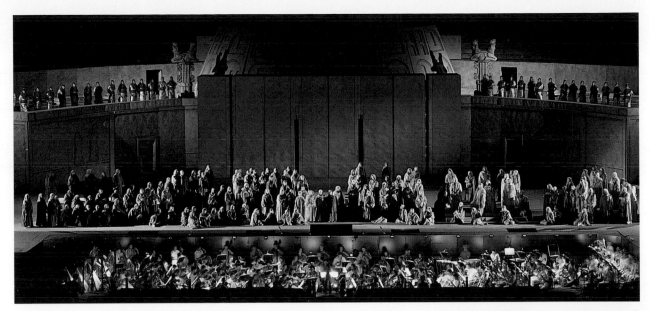

can be a crucial character in the drama. For example, in Benjamin Britten's *Peter Grimes*, an opera about a fisherman's ostracization from a tight-knit English fishing-village community, the chorus speaks with a terrifying unanimity in its condemnation of Grimes.

Verdi was a brilliant composer of operatic choral music. His chorus of the Hebrew Slaves from *Nabucco* (**CD track 23**) was so moving and rousing that it united the burgeoning movement for Italian unification into street cries of "VIVA V.E.R.D.I!" a punning acronym for "Viva Vittorio Emanuele Re D'Italia." But as with the ballet, it was the French and Russians — with their lavish tradition of grand opera — who really excelled in writing for the chorus. The mighty choruses in Mussorgsky's *Boris Godunov*, Berlioz's *Les Troyens*, Saint-Saëns' *Samson et Dalila* and Borodin's *Prince Igor* all spring to mind.

Wagner was reserved with his use of the chorus, believing on the whole that the chorus was dramatically artificial. In the twentieth century generally, the chorus has become less and less important.

The stage director

The director (sometimes called the producer in opera) is responsible for all the theatrical elements of a performance — from devising the overall style of the production, to rehearsing stage movements, discussing characterization with individual singers and interpreting the opera's

Top The celebrated chorus of the Hebrew Slaves from Verdi's first great national success, *Nabucco*, seen here at Verona. *Above* The Italian director Franco Zeffirelli rehearses Amy Shuard for a performance of *Cavalleria rusticana* and *I pagliacci* (by Mascagni and Leoncavallo respectively).

25

The staging of the four operas that make up Wagner's Ring Cycle is a vast undertaking for most opera houses, and is thus treated as a special event. The operas are open to many interpretations, offering the director a chance to do something new and often controversial. Pictured here are Rheinmaidens from four very different productions of the first opera of the Cycle, *Das Rheingold*, which appeared at (clockwise from right): the Scottish National Opera 1989 and London's Royal Opera House 1994, both directed by Richard Jones; the Metropolitan Opera House in New York, 1990, produced by Otto Schenk and Günther Schneider-Siemssen; and Berlin, 1906.

dramatic meaning in partnership with the conductor and the designer. While the director has emerged this century as an all-important figure in the operatic world (people now queue to see the latest production by a star director, irrespective of who is conducting or singing), this was not always the case. In the past, the task of operatic staging was handled by a leading actor or, later, by a stage manager. It was not until the second half of the nineteenth century, when Verdi and Wagner started to take an active role in the stage rehearsals of their works, that the whole concept of production began to develop as an important creative force in opera.

First-class directors can make their characters seem real, regardless of their costumes and settings, but the power of modern producers to interpret (some might say reinterpret and distort) the works of the great composers has led to many violent controversies in recent times. The British director Jonathan Miller, for example, has made it one of his specialities to update the setting of many of the operas he has produced. His famous production of *Rigoletto*, which moved the action from sixteenth-century Mantua to 1950s gangland New York, was a huge success. American producer, Peter Sellars, is both acclaimed and despised for his controversial updatings: under his direction, Mozart's *Così fan tutte* found its way into a neon-lit Los Angeles diner.

Other directors have been keen to obscure the sense of time and place in order to stress the universality of opera, or to mix costumes and sets from different ages. In a production of Wagner's Ring Cycle by the German director Nikolaus Lehnhoff, one scene featured Valhalla (home of the gods) as a model fairy-tale castle, which was followed by scenes of Wall Street skyscrapers, a middle-class domestic interior and a huge military installation.

Top Jonathan Miller (left) directs Gilbert and Sullivan's *The Mikado*, which he updated from imperial Japan to a 1920s hotel foyer. ***Above*** Peter Sellars (left) rehearses for Hindemith's *Mathis der Maler* which he moved from sixteenth-century Germany to a futuristic scaffolded cityscape.

Part of the pleasure of going to the opera is debating the merits of the production after the show. Of course, some productions may anger more than delight, but that is in the nature of opera. There is no right or wrong in modern staging. Producers can either choose to follow the directions laid down by the composer and the librettist, or they can ignore them. In the end, however, it all comes down to a question of entertainment. Was the production fun or powerful to watch? Did it help you enjoy the opera or, conversely, did it confuse or shock you?

Did you come away wanting to hear the music again? Do you think the production would have been enjoyed by the composer and librettist? These are the sorts of questions to ask yourself when assessing a new production; but, ultimately, if you could not understand what it was trying to do or say – even after reading the programme, learning about the opera and discussing the production with friends – then the director must have failed to some extent.

For those who are not well acquainted with opera it is as well to try to see conventional productions of the standard repertoire first before plunging into controversial reinterpretations. Among the most clear-sighted directors are Elijah Moshinsky, Götz Friedrich, Franco Zeffirelli, Graham Vick, John Cox, Peter Hall and Rudolf Hartmann.

The conductor and the orchestra

The conductor is arguably the most important figure in the opera house, for it is largely according to his or her strengths or weaknesses that a performance succeeds or fails. An opera conductor needs to have not only the necessary skills as a musician but an instinct for theatre; a sense of dramatic timing, as well as a knowledge of what is both musically and dramatically practical or appropriate.

Top Riccardo Muti conducts the orchestra at La Scala in Milan. *Above* The distinguished conductor Sir Georg Solti demonstrates dramatic passion to tenor Frank Lopardo, during rehearsals for Verdi's *La traviata*.

At the most fundamental level, though, the conductor's job is to coordinate the music and ensure that everybody sings and plays together on the night and that the balance of sound between the orchestra and soloists (as between the individual instruments themselves) is such that all can be clearly heard. Even before the rehearsals, a conscientious conductor will be involved at all levels of the production process, discussing with the designer and director every aspect of interpretation and presentation. Good opera conductors will also involve themselves in the training of soloists and chorus and the careful discussion of the music and characterization of the whole drama.

Working in an opera house orchestra can be a gruelling and thankless task. In many opera houses, where the orchestra is concealed in the pit, the players may not even be able to take a bow during the applause at the end. It is up to the conductor, therefore, to keep the players' concentration throughout a long performance – because if the orchestra stops concentrating, so does the audience.

Conductors often specialize in a certain repertoire and throughout this century each of the main opera composers has received special attention from individual conductors. Sir Charles Mackerras's famous performances of Janáček come to mind, as do Karl Böhm's performances of Richard Strauss and Mozart. Herbert von Karajan was another great Strauss conductor, but he also achieved notable success as an interpreter of Verdi and Wagner's music. Arturo Toscanini is most often associated with Italian repertoire, particularly Verdi and Puccini. Among the most distinguished of the modern opera conductors are James Levine, Daniel Barenboim, Bernard Haitink, Carlos Kleiber, Riccardo Muti, Georg Solti and Colin Davis.

Traditionally opera conductors have all been men but in recent years distinguished female conductors such as Simone Young, Sian Edwards and Anne Manson have emerged to prove that opera conducting is by no means an exclusively male skill.

The ballet

Ballet used to be an integral part of the opera performance, especially in France and Russia. As a rule the ballets served not to aid or sustain the drama but to act as some kind of *divertissement* from it. For instance, in an epic tragedy (the sort that were so popular with the French and Russian composers of "grand opera"), the introduction of ballet at appropriate moments would provide light relief for societies brought up on the idea that excessive emotion was vulgar and unrefined.

Composers such as Donizetti, Rossini and Verdi from Italy, where there was no tradition of dancing in opera, were usually forced to compose ballets for their operas if they wished them to be performed in Paris. The ballet in opera gradually fell out of fashion towards the end of the nineteenth century.

In many operas, ballet scenes form an essential and binding force. *Below* A young ballerina provides entertainment in Richard Strauss's *Capriccio*. *Centre* The St Petersburg Ball from Tchaikovsky's *Eugene Onegin*. *Bottom* Spanish dancing in Bizet's *Carmen*.

CHAPTER THREE

Behind the Scenes: the Making of an Opera

This chapter follows an opera company in the run-up to the revival in 1996 of a successful production of Mozart's *Die Zauberflöte* (The Magic Flute), originally produced in 1988 by the famous director Nicholas Hytner for English National Opera (ENO) in London.

Every busy international repertory company – from ENO in London to the Metropolitan Opera in New York – has an intricate and exhausting non-stop schedule getting its shows on to the stage. In a typical season from mid-September to early July, ENO will present nearly 200 performances of about eighteen operas. Eight of these operas will be new productions and the other ten will be revivals, in which popular past productions are remounted using the original sets and costumes, though often with different principals. While reviving a successful old production may not be as adventurous as staging a new one, revivals do have obvious advantages: they are easier and less expensive to mount, while the benefit of hindsight can be used to improve any details that didn't quite work the first time round.

The repertoire for each season is loosely planned five years in advance and firmed up three years in advance, when the director, designer, conductor and often the soloists are contracted and a budget set for each new production. The director and designer now need to

Left Sarastro and his priests on stage during a dress rehearsal. **Insets, from left** The conductor at a rehearsal; Pamina rehearsing with the orchestra; Monostatos being made up in his dressing room; the director on stage with three boys from the cast.

The model of the set for *Die Zauberflöte* is 25 times smaller than the real set. The technical department use the model to resolve potential problems, such as difficult scene changes.

decide on the particular look and feel of their production. A year before the opening night, the designer presents a scaled model of the set, plus costumes designs, and talks the company through the design of the production scene by scene. A lighting plan is submitted by the lighting designer some time later. The model is scrutinized by the production team for its cost and practicality, and by the conductor in case it presents acoustic problems. After the model has been approved, the director and designer may need to revise the budget to bring production costs down. Preparations for the opera continue over the next twelve months, with the set-builders beginning work on a life-size version of the set (using the model as a reference) and the wardrobe department transforming the costume designs into workable patterns. Rehearsals begin in earnest about four or five weeks before the opening night.

THE OPERA HOUSE CAST

Director and revival director
The role of the director is discussed in full on pages 25–28. It is rare for the original director to come back each time a production is remounted, so a revival director will be appointed to recreate the original, preserving the spirit of the first production (any major changes would require permission from the original director). The revival director is helped by the so-called "bible," which contains very detailed notes of the original staging.

Staff director
Assists the director/revival director and is responsible for rehearsing the understudies and ensuring the best possible artistic standard is maintained throughout the run of performances; often entrusted with directing future revivals.

Conductor
While most repertory companies have their own resident conductors, guest conductors are regularly invited to conduct. See also pages 28–29.

Assistant conductor
Collaborates with the conductor and takes some rehearsals.

Other musical staff
A chorus master usually rehearses the chorus while the conductor works with the soloists. Both chorus and principals may have some training with a vocal coach.

Designer (sets and costumes)
Working with the director, the designer conceptualizes the look of the production and provides designs that in-house staff then use to make the real sets and costumes. Some big chorus productions have their own costume designers.

Technical director
In charge of all the technical departments.

Production manager and assistant
The production team is responsible, among other things, for translating the model on to the real stage and ensuring each aspect of the production works, on and off stage.

Stage management team
Manages and coordinates all rehearsals and performances.

Stage department
Looks after the scene changes: getting sets, props and people on and off stage.

Lighting department
Lighting technicians operate the lights and put into practice the plans of the lighting designer.

Props department
The team that makes the props for each production.

Wardrobe and millinery department
Includes the head of wardrobe, wardrobe supervisors, cloth dyers, cutters and makers, as well as hat-makers.

Wig department
The wig-making department is responsible not only for manufacturing wigs for every member of the cast, but also any false beards, moustaches and noses.

Transport and storage department
Responsible for moving and storing the sets and props.

Administrative staff
A repertory company is supported by a huge staff in artistic administration, finance, sales and front of house management.

Studio rehearsals

Directors generally begin to plan the details of the staging well before the first rehearsals. Early rehearsals, with a piano accompanist, take place in a studio away from the opera house, with the director and the conductor respectively supervising dramatic and musical matters. Rehearsals are a gruelling process, held morning and afternoon, often six days a week. Studio rehearsals last three to six weeks. For this revival, Act I is polished in the first week, and Act II in the second, while the third week is used to run both acts together. Meanwhile, separate orchestral and choral rehearsals take place with the conductor and chorus master, sometimes involving the principals.

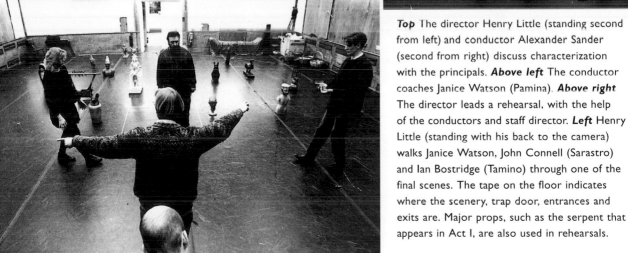

Top The director Henry Little (standing second from left) and conductor Alexander Sander (second from right) discuss characterization with the principals. **Above left** The conductor coaches Janice Watson (Pamina). **Above right** The director leads a rehearsal, with the help of the conductors and staff director. **Left** Henry Little (standing with his back to the camera) walks Janice Watson, John Connell (Sarastro) and Ian Bostridge (Tamino) through one of the final scenes. The tape on the floor indicates where the scenery, trap door, entrances and exits are. Major props, such as the serpent that appears in Act I, are also used in rehearsals.

The sitzprobe

There will be at least two musical rehearsals before moving to the stage, involving the full cast, chorus and orchestra, conductor. These rehearsals are known as *sitzprobes*, German for "seated rehearsals," and take place either in the theatre or at a large studio. The *sitzprobe* often brings together for the first time the soloists, chorus and orchestra, and the conductor will use the opportunity to thoroughly rehearse the music without the distraction of lighting, props, costumes and movements.

Top left Nicola Sharkey (Queen of the Night) sings with the orchestra during a *sitzprobe*. **Above** *Die Zauberflöte* has parts for three young boys, here rehearsing during a *sitzprobe*. **Left** The conductor instructs the orchestra to drop the volume.

Preparations backstage: sets and props

Three weeks before the first night, revival sets are brought out of storage and sent to the theatre, where invariably it is discovered that small adjustments and repairs need to be made. In a repertory company like English National Opera, different operas run nearly every night so sets need to be dismantled, transported and stored two or three times a day. The first stage rehearsal usually takes place in the evening and will be attended by production, props and wardrobe managers who check everything is in good working order.

Above Transported daily to and from the warehouse in which it is stored, the set is unloaded by stage technicians.

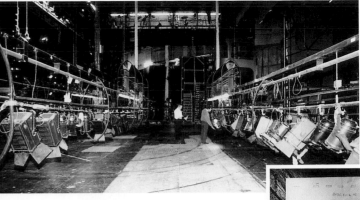

Left Stage technicians help to construct part of the huge set. Above Members of the lighting crew change the coloured gels of the lights. The lighting for this production is complicated by the mirrored floor. Right The lighting plan for *Die Zauberflöte*. Lighting at the London Coliseum is controlled by a computerized lighting console.

Preparations backstage: costumes and wigs

The cast will be measured about twelve weeks before the opening night for costumes and wigs, which are then fitted and adjusted throughout the studio rehearsal period. They should be finished in time for the first stage rehearsal. There are cunning ways of designing original costumes so they can be adjusted later to fit any singer, but a few may need to be completely remade for a revival.

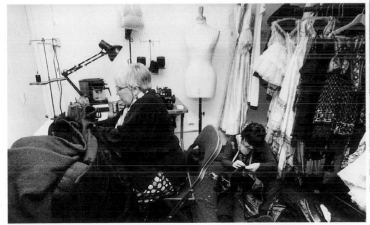

Above Putting the finishing touches to a costume. The challenge for the wardrobe department is to transform the original designs into wearable items of clothing. Right Wigs in a special drying machine.

The stage rehearsals

For the chorus and soloists the weeks of rehearsal are almost at an end and it is time, with only one or two weeks to go before the first night, to move out of the rehearsal studio and on to the stage. The transition is not always easy: the cast now has to work with the real sets, props and costumes, many of them for the first time. Singers also have to adjust their voices to the acoustics of the huge auditorium and their movements to the size of the stage, which may be larger than the rehearsal studio. It is a nerve-racking time for everyone, not least for the technical department who have been working, as often as not through the night, to complete the costumes, wigs, props and sets. Stage rehearsals are divided into those organized by the director (with piano accompaniment only) and those called by the conductor employing the full orchestra.

Because this production is extremely complex technically the stage rehearsals are very important for the technical department – which has only a week to master the lighting, sound and scene changes before the opening night. **Top** The stage manager on stage with Janice Watson. **Above left** A deputy stage manager in the prompt corner follows the score in order to give the cues. **Above right** The director, staff director and conductor watch a rehearsal from the stalls. **Right** View of the stage and orchestra pit during a piano rehearsal.

Above left Sally Harrison (playing Papagena) being lowered down in her nest from the flies. **Top right** The show manager and head of technical services on stage after a rehearsal. **Above centre** This production features five doves, here shown with their trainer. **Above right** A member of the orchestra cleans the reed of his clarinet. **Left** The mirrored floor of the stage has to be cleaned after every performance. The cast wear shoes with specially made soles to avoid slipping.

The general or dress rehearsal

Although all stage rehearsals should be in costume, the dress rehearsal (two days before the first night) is sometimes the only opportunity to run through the opera from start to finish with no interruptions and with everything in place, as it would be for a performance. The conductor, director, technicians, understudies and sometimes an audience of friends are present. The principals usually have a day off following the dress rehearsal, but the chorus and orchestra often have another opera to perform. The set is erected overnight before the first performance, so it is ready for technical work the next day.

Below right Penelope Walmsley-Clark, one of the Three Ladies, puts the finishing touches to her makeup, following the plan (*right*) designed by the makeup department.
Below left A dresser helps a dancer into his bear costume.

Above The schedule of intensive rehearsals begins to take its toll on Ian Bostridge (playing the lead, Tamino), who uses an inhaler in his dressing room to alleviate the symptoms of a cold.

Above Tamino on stage with the three boys during the dress rehearsal. After the rehearsal is over the conductor and director will give notes to the cast about any necessary adjustments.

Postmortems are held after the dress rehearsal has finished. **Left** The director, staff director and technical managers meet on stage. **Below** The technical staff convene in the stalls bar to resolve any outstanding problems.

The opening night

The latest revival of *Die Zauberflöte* opens at last to great critical acclaim. After each performance the costumes are removed to be washed, the floor is polished and the sets are taken down and transported to the warehouse. Meanwhile the set for the opera being rehearsed the next morning is constructed overnight. An opera is never performed on two consecutive nights as soloists usually need to rest their voices for a day.

REVIEWS
"...if you are lucky enough to see a production as beautifully done as Nicholas Hytner's 1988 staging for English National Opera, newly revived by Henry Little, the three hours or so pass in a flash" *Sunday Express*
"...so splendidly performed that it is a joy every inch of the way" *Daily Express*
"Alexander Sander's stylish conducting is the perfect springboard for exceptional singing" *The Times*

Left The curtain call at the end of the opera, with Papageno and Papagena sitting happily in their nest full of chicks. **Above** On stage after the curtain has come down, Dennis Marks – General Director of English National Opera – congratulates Ian Bostridge on his performance.

CHAPTER FOUR
The Story of Opera

Opera is a play in which the drama is conveyed predominantly by music and song rather than by speech. *Dafne* (1597) – by the Roman-born composer Jacopo Peri and the Florentine poet, Ottavio Rinuccini – was the first real work of this kind and a typical product of the Italian Renaissance. Peri and Rinuccini were members of a group of artists and thinkers known as the *Camerata* (club or society), established in Florence at the end of the sixteenth century to produce a new art form that would draw its inspiration from the tragic dramas of the ancient Greeks and Romans. Unfortunately, the music for *Dafne* has long since disappeared and only the text now survives, but Rinuccini and Peri's drama (in which the beautiful Dafne is transformed into a laurel tree) was clearly a success at the time, for in the years following its 1597 premiere at a private house in Florence, new operas started to appear all over Italy. Peri and Rinuccini were soon commissioned for more. Their *Euridice*, composed to celebrate the marriage of Henri IV of France and Marie de' Medici, is the earliest opera for which the music still survives.

Today the most popular opera of the early seventeenth century is undoubtedly Monteverdi's *L'Orfeo*, composed some ten years after *Dafne* and first performed in 1607. Extracts from this opera can be heard on **CD tracks 6** and **24**. Two other operas by Monteverdi have remained in the popular modern repertory, *Il ritorno d'Ulisse in patria* (1640) and *L'incoronazione di Poppea* (1643). Both works are longer

Opposite Lionized and adored, Farinelli (1705–82) was the leading soprano-castrato of his time. Through his long career he amassed a fortune and eventually retired to a luxurious villa near Bologna in 1759 where he was visited by Mozart, Gluck, Casanova and the Holy Roman Emperor, Joseph II.

than *L'Orfeo* and, for the beginner at least, less approachable. In fact, some scholars are now suggesting that Monteverdi may not have been the composer of *Poppea* after all.

Because opera was such an expensive entertainment, performances were reserved at first for special occasions, when the entire costs were usually met by a wealthy prince or potentate. The Church generally disapproved of opera and was not involved. It was not long, though, before the excitement of the new art form had spread to a wider and increasingly enthusiastic audience. By the middle of the seventeenth century, purpose-built opera houses for the general public were being erected in many of the major Italian cities. By 1690, some cities – Venice, for instance – were endowed with more than half a dozen opera houses. The scenery was always spectacular and there was no end to the ingenuity of the special-effects men of the Baroque age. It is no wonder that the lure of this extravagant new entertainment was soon to spread from Italy right across the whole of Europe.

A herbaceous stage set for a lavish French court production of Lully's opera, *Atys*, in 1676.

Beyond the borders of Italy

Opera remained an Italian import in most countries during the seventeenth century. It was almost always sung in Italian, usually by Italian singers, with many composers learning their trade in Italy. But tastes varied across Europe and the settings of operas began to move from the stylized formalities of Classical legend to tragic and even comic subjects of a more human nature to accord with local fashion.

The two great centres for opera outside Italy were Vienna, where the imperial court was reputed to have staged some of the most lavish productions of the age, and Paris, where the French composers developed their own brand of opera-ballet that grew out of the long tradition of French court entertainment but was also influenced by Italian developments. The leading composer in France during the seventeenth century was Jean-Baptiste Lully, who ironically was Italian-born. Court composer to King Louis XIV, he set his operas in French rather than Italian, and although Italian was

to remain the most fashionable operatic language right through to the end of the eighteenth century, other non-Italian composers had begun to look to their own native languages by the end of the seventeenth century. In 1678 an opera company was started in Hamburg where Reinhard Keiser was the leading composer of opera in German. His works, which made a strong impression on the young Handel when he visited the city of Hamburg in 1703, are still occasionally performed today.

England's greatest composer of the time was Henry Purcell. *Dido and Aeneas* (1689) was his only opera in the strict sense and was set to an English libretto by Nahum Tate (*pages 56–59* and **CD tracks 28** and **29**). He also composed a number of semi-operas – spoken plays that incorporated musical masques with spectacular visual displays – but these are seldom staged today in the grand spirit in which they were conceived.

Handel and his contemporaries

There are only two opera composers from the early eighteenth century whose works are regularly performed around the world today: George Frideric Handel, whose large output of operas is all in Italian, and Jean-Philippe Rameau, who continued in Paris the tradition of Lully with balletic operas in French. Handel lived and worked for most of his adult life in London and had to struggle with an ever-dwindling English enthusiasm for Italian opera. John Gay's *The Beggar's Opera* (1728), for instance, was an English ballad opera about lowlife London crooks that used popular tunes of the day arranged by John Pepusch to an English libretto. It was first presented by the promoter John Rich at Lincoln's Inn Fields, London and its success was so enormous and immediate that it was said to have made "Rich gay and Gay rich." Perhaps *The Beggar's Opera* should be seen more as a forerunner to the musicals of Broadway and the West End than a crucial cog in the history of developing opera, but

Left The leading composer in seventeenth-century France: Jean-Baptiste Lully *Below* A portrait of George Frideric Handel. *Bottom* A scene from Handel's opera *Alcina* produced at the Royal Opera House, London.

43

Above Marilyn Horne sings the title role of Handel's *Rinaldo* at the Metropolitan Opera House, New York, in 1984. Today the role is more often sung by a male countertenor.

Below An anonymous Dutch engraving, *c.* 1770, of Orfeo in Hades, from Gluck's opera *Orfeo ed Euridice*.

either way it turned out to be a nail in the coffin for Handel, Giovanni Bononcini and others who were trying to promote serious Italian opera in London at the time.

Handel's forty or so operas are often criticized for the structure of their arias (known as *da capo* arias), whose long repeats arrest the progress of the drama – a criticism that may partly explain the neglect of all his operas for nearly 160 years after his death in 1759. Eighteenth-century opera was dominated by the extraordinary voices of castrati (*see page 24*) and Handel was not alone in composing much of his music for the specific voices of the great castrated Italian singers of the time. At their best, Handel's operas (**CD tracks 9** and **18**) are laden with intense human feeling and, in the musical portrayal of powerful emotions like anger, sorrow, madness and anguish, they must be considered equal to any of the great operas of the nineteenth century.

Rameau's operas are notable for the excitement and quick imagination of the music and, unlike those by Handel, are rich with choral music and lively interludes for ballet. *Platée* (1745), *Anacréon* (1754), *Les Indes galantes* (1735) and *Castor et Pollux* (1737) are the most frequently performed operas by Rameau today.

We should not forget that Italy's leading opera composer of the time, Alessandro Scarlatti (whose stage works are now rarely, if ever, performed), should rightly be considered the father of modern opera. It was Scarlatti, after all, who realized the importance of the aria for conveying poetic operatic emotions, and he also developed the distinction between ordinary recitative, which is accompanied only by harpsichord (*recitativo secco* or dry recitative) for ordinary dialogue, and recitative accompanied by the orchestra (*recitativo stromentato* or, more commonly, *recitativo accompagnato*) to awaken stronger emotions.

The reformers: Gluck and Mozart

Two towering figures dominate our view of opera in the second half of the eighteenth century: Christoph Willibald von Gluck and Wolfgang Amadeus Mozart. Gluck, a German composer of Bohemian descent, strove to reform the operatic art that, he believed, was in danger of stagnating. In his view arias had become showpieces for virtuoso singers and little more. Gluck escaped from traditional formalities and created a new, more vital, intensely expressive drama in which the music and the words were more closely allied than ever before. Gluck's greatest operas – *Orfeo ed Euridice* (1762), *Alceste* (1767), *Iphigénie en Aulide* (1774) and *Armide* (1777), some of which were composed in French, others in Italian – not only paved the way for the great masterpieces of Mozart in the years that followed but also remained a seminal influence on other composers in the nineteenth century, particularly Berlioz. An extract from Gluck's most famous aria "Che farò senza Euridice?" (from *Orfeo*) is on **CD track 25**.

Mozart's great achievement as an opera composer was his innovative ability to define character through his music. His three best-loved operas, all to librettos by Lorenzo Da Ponte, are *Le nozze di Figaro* (1786, **CD track 20**), *Don Giovanni* (1787, *pages 62–67* and **CD tracks 4, 30 and 31**) and *Così fan tutte* (1790). Mozart's complex and yet spontaneous music set new challenges for generations of opera composers to come. In his lifetime he achieved instant popularity with his German operas, *Die Entführung aus dem Serail* (The Abduction from the Seraglio, 1782) and *Die Zauberflöte* (The Magic Flute, 1791, **CD track 15**), but his last opera, *La clemenza di Tito* (The Clemency of Titus, 1791), composed in a few short weeks at the very end of his life, has never been as popular.

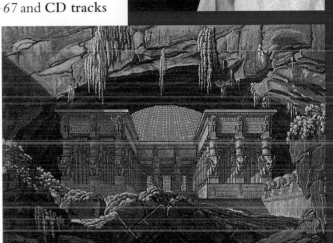

New forms of Italian opera: bel canto and verismo

The Italians loved vocal virtuosity and enjoyed hearing singers trilling and embellishing their parts, even though the style of music often had very little to do with the words they were supposed to be singing. Gioacchino Rossini was one of the first Italian composers to write out all his trills and decorations, but for well over a hundred years before that it was up to individual singers to improvise whatever virtuosic flourishes they felt were appropriate. Rossini is most admired for his comic operas or *opera buffa* such as *Il barbiere di Siviglia* (*see pages 70–77*,

Top Geraint Evans and Elisabeth Schwarzkopf as Figaro and Susanna in the first scene of Mozart's *Le nozze di Figaro* (The Marriage of Figaro). *Above* Set design for Act II of Mozart's *Die Zauberflöte* (The Magic Flute) dating from 1816, twenty-five years after Mozart's death.

CD tracks **32** and **33**), for which his bubbly, light and quick-witted style of composition is admirably suited. His tragedies are often criticized for their musical superficiality. Certainly for a modern audience used to the grand passions of Giuseppe Verdi and Giacomo Puccini, these works can seem a little lightweight.

Rossini was a leading composer of the *bel canto* style. In fact he was probably responsible for coining the phrase when, in 1858, he inveighed against modern Italian singers complaining: "Alas for us, we have lost our bel canto." The term literally means "beautiful singing," but it is widely used to describe a particular school of Italian opera best exemplified by the works of Gaetano Donizetti, Vincenzo Bellini and, to a certain extent, Verdi.

According to Rossini, a *bel canto* voice must possess an even tone throughout its range and an effortless delivery of highly florid music. To attain these, Rossini believed, required long and careful training, but the style itself could not be taught – only assimilated by listening to the greatest Italian exponents. At its best the *bel canto* style is riveting and exhilarating. Bellini's *Norma* (1831) and *I Puritani* (1835) both offer fine examples of what is meant by *bel canto* in the decorative flights of the principal soprano roles (**CD track 26** features an extract from the great aria *bel canto* "Casta diva" from *Norma*, sung by Jane Eaglen). Donizetti's style is more extrovert than that of Bellini. His tragedy, *Lucia di Lammermoor* (1835, **CD track 3**), in which the heroine is driven mad after being cruelly deceived, affords perhaps the best introduction to Donizetti's robust style of Romantic *bel canto*.

The cover of a special edition of *L'illustrazione italiana* devoted to *Falstaff* – Verdi's last opera (but only one of two comedies), which was first performed in 1893.

Verdi's impact on Italian opera in the nineteenth century was so colossal that no other Italian opera composer of the time could have enjoyed working in his shadow. From the time of his first big national success with *Nabucco* in 1842 until his last opera, *Falstaff* of 1893, Verdi was unchallenged for the title of Italy's greatest living composer. He strove perhaps more than any other opera composer to inject his works with characterizations that were both sympathetic and realistic and to imbue opera with the same vibrancy and urgency as the best spoken theatre. With each successive work, Verdi took further strides to achieve his goal, and appeared, even in his late seventies, to be discovering novel means of expression with a new, more fluid and less extravagant musical language (*see pages 78–85*, **CD tracks 7, 13, 14, 16, 22, 23, 34 and 35**).

Giacomo Puccini was Verdi's successor as the leading Italian opera composer in the last years of the nineteenth century. In common with Verdi, he believed in the absolute power of melody and remained, to the end, a resolutely anti-modernist composer. His music is notable for its flowing melodies, melting harmonies and rich orchestration, so ideally suited to the passions of his principal characters. Puccini loosely belonged to a group of Italian composers known as the *verismo* or realist school. In essence, *verismo* composers aimed to bring lowlife characters on to the opera stage – instead of the lofty figures of previous centuries – and present their rawest emotions in a compelling and realistic context. The idea was not of course entirely new: we have already mentioned *The Beggar's Opera* of 1728, but perhaps Verdi's *La traviata* (1853), the story of a consumptive Parisian courtesan, or Bizet's *Carmen* (1875, *pages 104–9*, **CD tracks 40 and 41**), the rough adventures of a sensual Spanish gypsy, should be cited as forerunners to the Italian *verismo* movement. What really made *verismo* popular was the mixture of loud, powerfully tuneful music accompanying passionate tales of sex and violence. Examples of Puccini's rich musical style can be found on **CD tracks 2, 27, 42 and 43**. Aside from Puccini, the most popular composers of the *verismo* school were Pietro Mascagni, Ruggiero Leoncavallo and Umberto Giordano.

German Romantic opera

At the beginning of the nineteenth century opera was reaching out to increasingly middle-class audiences and the fashion for opera sung in Italian was giving way to popular demand for native languages and more operatic realism. Ludwig van Beethoven's *Fidelio* (1805–14,

Top Title page of a score for four scenes from Puccini's opera *La Bohème*. **Above** Portrait of the great German composer, Ludwig van Beethoven.

47

Top Welsh soprano Gwyneth Jones as Leonore and Spas Wenkoff as Florestan in a production of Beethoven's only opera, *Fidelio*, at San Francisco. *Above* A scene from Act IV of Glinka's second opera *Ruslan and Lyudmila* – one of the founding works of Russian nationalist "grand opera" – performed at the Kirov Opera in St Petersburg.

CD track 10) is a great hymn to humanity, conjugal love, fidelity and political freedom. Though partly comic, it is essentially a work of idealism. To many, *Fidelio* is the greatest opera ever written, while others consider it to be more of a dramatic cantata than an opera. German Romantic opera, based on stories from German history and legend, flourished at this time with the works of Carl Maria von Weber and E.T.A. Hoffmann. A generation later, a popular taste had developed for comic operas sung in German, with those of Gustav Lortzing, Otto Nicolai and Friedrich von Flotow proving particularly successful.

Wagner was undoubtedly the most influential composer of the nineteenth century and also the most controversial. His contribution to opera in both theoretical and practical terms was enormous. He expanded the opera house orchestra, introducing new instruments and greater numbers of players; he revolutionized the expressive use of harmony; he brought greater length and intensity to opera than ever before; and he eschewed most of the traditional opera formalities (arias, ensembles and ballets for instance). He aspired to what he called *Gesamtkunstwerk* or "complete artwork," in which he hoped to produce a perfect aesthetic synthesis of poetry, music, drama and design. Examples of Wagner's music can be heard on CD tracks 5, 11, 12, 19, 36 and 37. He even built his own theatre at Bayreuth to stage his productions. Of all the remarkable creations by this remarkable man, the four operas of *Der Ring des Nibelungen* (1869–76), known as the Ring Cycle, surely stand out as his most revolutionary achievement.

Operatic nationalism

Despite the enormous influence of Verdi and Wagner, composers outside Italy and Germany established their own styles and traditions, particularly in Russia (where tastes developed for a nationalist opera of epic histories or fairy tales, dealing principally with love and heroism) and France. The French also had a predilection for great spectacles, with huge crowd scenes, elaborate scenery and epic stories, which is why French opera of the nineteenth century came to be known as "grand opera." Mikhail Glinka is regarded as the father of Russian musical nationalism and his influence on composers such as Aleksandr

Borodin, Nikolai Rimsky-Korsakov, Modest Mussorgsky (*pages 96–103*, **CD tracks 38** and **39**) and Pyotr Ilyich Tchaikovsky was immense. Glinka introduced Russian folk melody into opera, giving a characteristic Russian feel to all his music. Tchaikovsky, Borodin and Mussorgsky brought an intensely personal and psychological angle into the framework of epic "grand opera."

The French, meanwhile, continued to develop the lavish and large-scale traditions of French opera handed down to them from Rameau and Gluck. The Italian-born composer Gaspare Spontini was an influential figure in Paris in the early nineteenth century. So too were André Grétry, Daniel Auber, Etienne-Nicolas Méhul and Adrien Boieldieu, but the overriding genius of the period was Hector Berlioz, whose great comedy *Benvenuto Cellini* (1838) and five-act Virgilian tragedy *Les Troyens* (1856–58) are now regarded as the finest achievements of the French "grand opera" tradition. In terms

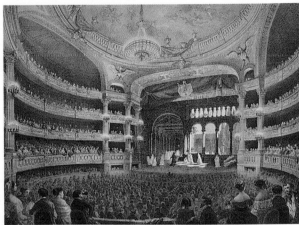

Below A painting of an 1840s production of Meyerbeer's *Robert le Diable* at the Paris Opéra. **Bottom** A set design for Rimsky-Korsakov's last opera, *The Golden Cockerel*.

Below The title page of a piano score for Richard Strauss's *Salome*. **Bottom** The front cover of the score of Alban Berg's opera, *Wozzeck*.

of contemporary popularity, however, Jacques Halévy and Giacomo Meyerbeer were more successful. The tradition continued into the later nineteenth century with many operas that have remained firm favourites ever since: Charles Gounod's *Faust* (1859), Georges Bizet's *Carmen* (1875) and Camille Saint-Saëns' *Samson et Dalila* (1877). But the most successful of all Romantic French opera composers, in his own time at least, was Jules Massenet (**CD track 1**). The luscious style and rich melodic charm that he employed for a wide variety of tragedies and comedies earned him a considerable fortune.

In Czechoslovakia, Antonin Dvořák and Bedřich Smetana were forming their own brand of Czech nationalist opera that fell somewhere between the Russian and Italian schools.

Opera in the twentieth century

In opera, as in all art forms, the early twentieth century was a time for experimentation and fragmentation. The old schools gave way to individuals hoping to create something different, something bold and new. Claude Debussy, the great precursor of modern music, drew much of his inspiration for his only completed opera, *Pelléas et Mélisande* (1902), from Wagner's *Parsifal* (1882), but even so it was a strikingly innovative work.

One thing that all early twentieth-century opera composers seem to have agreed upon was that opera had to change if it was to live into the new century. Still, the essential artificiality of opera continued to vex composers. Béla Bartók, Arnold Schoenberg and Franz Shreker attempted to explore psychology on almost Freudian lines. This approach was most successfully adopted by Richard Strauss, the last of the late Romantics. Strauss delves deep into the human psyche, portraying his heroines with a masterful musical insight ranging from the touching vulnerability of the Marschallin in *Der Rosenkavalier* (1911) to the terrifying insanity of *Salome* (1905). Alban Berg pushed the point even further in his two operas *Wozzeck* (1925) and *Lulu* (unfinished at his death in 1935), with characterizations that are wild and extreme. Several decades later, the English composer Benjamin Britten wrote operas specializing in the psychology of loneliness, in which the leading

character was often ostracized or reviled by the society in which he lived. While Puccini and his Czech contemporary Leoš Janáček continued to develop their own distinctive forms of *verismo*, other composers, most notably Francis Poulenc in *Les Mamelles de Tirésias* (1947) and Dmitri Shostokovich in *The Nose* (1930), experimented with surrealism and poetic nonsense. Igor Stravinsky's only full length opera, *The Rake's Progress* (1951), set to an English libretto by W.H. Auden and Chester Kallman, is an important work of neoclassicism, returning for its inspiration to some of the traditional forms and set-pieces of Gluck, Mozart and other Classical composers.

The late twentieth century has seen a sad decline in the popularity of new opera. The fault lies mostly with the composers, many of whom have moved too far away from the expectations of their audiences. Complex ugly music, layer upon layer of impenetrable symbolism and pseudo-intellectual posturing have meant that most modern commissions have never been revived. There are of course exceptions. Philip Glass in America has produced genuinely successful operas, so too have Michael Tippett from England and Hans Werner Henze from Germany, but too many contemporary composers are still desperately in need of a means to communicate with modern audiences, a means that needs to be both new and, at the same time, intelligibly entertaining.

Top A scene from Stravinsky's opera *The Rake's Progress* at Glyndebourne in England. The set for this production was designed by David Hockney. **Above** *The Cave* was American composer Steve Reich's vision of how modern opera might develop. The voices were sampled and the words displayed on a screen.

CHAPTER FIVE

The World of Opera through Eight Masterworks

Knowing what to listen to in an opera is often one of the most confusing aspects of the art form. Should we be concentrating on the voices or the orchestra? How can we follow more than one character singing at the same time? What should we be listening for in a particular voice? How important is phrasing? This chapter explores how to get more from opera by looking at – and listening to – the work of eight of the most celebrated opera composers: Purcell, Mozart, Rossini, Verdi, Wagner, Mussorgsky, Bizet and Puccini. Their works span more than three centuries and five languages. One opera by each composer is discussed in detail. These eight operas have been chosen because they are representative not only of their composer's finest work but also of a wider operatic style. The works thus range from early English Baroque through Italian tragedy and comedy, Wagnerian music-drama and Russian "grand opera" to French *opéra comique* and classic Italian *verismo*.

The text gives a synopsis of the plot, the story behind the opera (who commissioned it and so on) and biographies of the composer and librettist, as well as exploring the musical highlights of the opera. A key song from each work is featured in full on the accompanying CD, and decoded moment by moment on the "timeline" which explains what to listen for and when. Musical highlights, corresponding to the timings on your CD counter, are annotated at key points above the timeline, while a computerized image of the music, working on the same

Opposite A scene from Rossini's *Il barbiere di Siviglia* (The Barber of Seville), one of the eight masterworks featured in this chapter.

principles as a cardiograph, visualizes the rise and fall of volume. Coloured bars (the colour depending on the type of voice – *see table opposite*) show at a glance who is singing and when. The text of each song is printed below the timeline, so you can follow the words the characters are singing using the key words above the coloured bars. An extract from another highlight from each opera is also featured on the CD, illustrating a different aspect of the work.

If you enjoy the two extracts from the operas, it is well worth listening to a complete recording. Alternatively, try to see a video of each opera or, better still, a live performance – all of these works are regularly performed at opera houses around the world. Further recommendations for where to go next follow the discussion of each opera, as well as synopses of some of the other major operas by each composer.

HOW THE TIMELINES WORK

The time (given in minutes and seconds) corresponds with the time shown on the CD counter.

Annotations guide you through each song moment by moment, showing what to listen for and when.

Instruments in grey indicate when they are important to the orchestral accompaniment.

The colour of each bar denotes the type of voice (*see table opposite*); the length of the bar shows how long each character is singing for. The key words above the bars indicate what each character is singing.

The heartbeat-like ribbon shows the volume of the music. Long lines denote loud music and short lines denote quiet music.

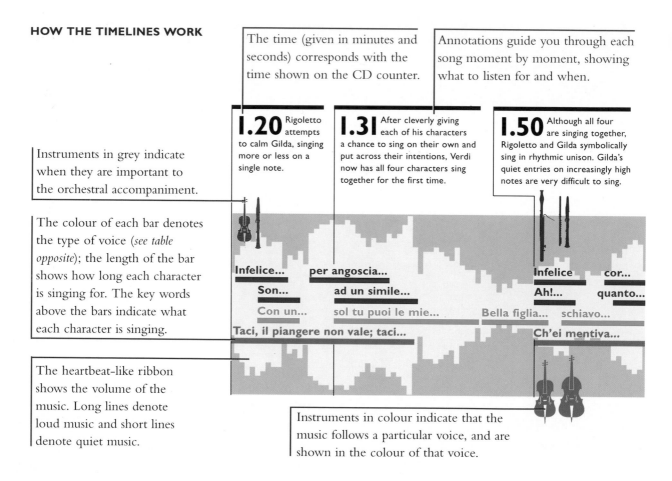

1.20 Rigoletto attempts to calm Gilda, singing more or less on a single note.

1.31 After cleverly giving each of his characters a chance to sing on their own and put across their intentions, Verdi now has all four characters sing together for the first time.

1.50 Although all four are singing together, Rigoletto and Gilda symbolically sing in rhythmic unison. Gilda's quiet entries on increasingly high notes are very difficult to sing.

Infelice...   per angoscia...   Infelice...   cor...
Son...   ad un simile...   Ah!...   quanto...
Con un...   sol tu puoi le mie...   Bella figlia...   schiavo...
Taci, il piangere non vale; taci...   Ch'ei mentiva...

Instruments in colour indicate that the music follows a particular voice, and are shown in the colour of that voice.

THE TYPES OF VOICE FEATURED IN THE TIMELINES

■ **Soprano** Dido (*Dido and Aeneas*), Zerlina (*Don Giovanni*), Gilda (*Rigoletto*), Eva (*Die Meistersinger*), Tosca

■ **Mezzo-soprano** Carmen

■ **Contralto** Maddalena (*Rigoletto*)

■ **Tenor** Duke of Mantua (*Rigoletto*), Walther (*Die Meistersinger*), Prince Shuisky (*Boris Godunov*)

■ **Baritone** Don Giovanni, Figaro (*Il Barbiere di Siviglia*), Rigoletto

■ **Bass-baritone** Hans Sachs (*Die Meistersinger*)

■ **Bass** Boris Godunov

■ **Chorus** *Die Meistersinger, Boris Godunov, Carmen*

■ **Male chorus** *Die Meistersinger, Boris Godunov*

INSTRUMENTS FEATURED IN THE TIMELINES

violin
viola
cello
double-bass

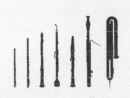

piccolo
flute
oboe
cor anglais
clarinet
bassoon
double-bassoon

trumpet
trombone
French horn
tuba

harp
harpsichord
timpani (kettle drum)
bass drum

bell
tambourine
triangle
tam-tam (gong)

PURCELL:
DIDO AND AENEAS

CD tracks 28 (timeline) and 29

Opera in *three acts*
Music by *Henry Purcell*
Libretto by *Nahum Tate* after *Virgil's* Aeneid
Original language *English*
First performed in *London, 1689*
Approximate length *60 minutes*

Dido and Aeneas is generally considered to be the greatest English-language opera written before the twentieth century. It is also the only true opera that Purcell ever wrote. Purcell spent much of his short life composing incidental music for many plays, as well as a series of semi-operas (works that combined spoken dialogue with grand and spectacular episodes of song, orchestral music and ballet) that were all successful in his lifetime. Unlike most operas of the Baroque age, which had happy endings, *Dido and Aeneas* is a tragedy. The pain and suffering depicted in the final aria, Dido's Lament, are extraordinary. The whole opera lasts just one hour and serves as a splendid and easily accessible entrée not only into the music of this wonderful composer but also into the operatic and vocal conventions of his time.

Summary of the plot

Having survived the Trojan War, the Trojan prince Aeneas and his men flee the wreckage of the city of Troy to fulfil their destinies by founding a new city at Rome. Blown off course, however, they land on the North African coast at Carthage, where they are entertained by

Lena Nordin as Dido and Perarne Wahlgren as Aeneas in a production of Purcell's opera at Drottningholm in Sweden.

Dido, the Queen of Carthage. The opera opens with Dido feeling leaden-hearted and downcast, being overburdened by affairs of state and other matters. A love affair soon develops between the Trojan prince and his beautiful Carthaginian hostess, Queen Dido, much to the general elation of her courtiers. But Aeneas's compelling sense of destiny, stirred up by the evil meddlings of a disenchanted sorceress (the librettist Nahum Tate's main departure from Virgil), drives him away from Carthage in order to found a new Trojan city. Dido, left behind, is too distraught for comforting and shortly dies of a broken heart, mourned by a chorus of cupids.

A brief history of the opera

Purcell's *Dido and Aeneas* was modelled to some extent on an earlier work, *Venus and Adonis* (described as a "Masque for the Entertainment of the King in Three Acts"), by his teacher John Blow. Like *Venus and Adonis*, *Dido* was performed at Josias Priest's Boarding School for Young Gentlewomen in Chelsea, London with an all female cast, probably in the spring of 1689. Whether this (the only known performance during Purcell's lifetime) was actually the world premiere is still a matter of debate. It is possible that the work formed part of the celebrations for the joint coronation of William and Mary on 11 April 1689 (perhaps prior to the Boarding School performance), and according to one scholar at least it may have been performed to Queen Mary herself at this time. The opera's original prologue, to which the music has been lost, alluded to William and Mary and praised the advent of spring. On stylistic grounds, scholars are prepared to concede that the opera could have been composed in 1685 or even earlier.

Dido's Lament and other highlights

The most striking feature of Dido's Lament ("When I am laid in earth:" **CD track 28**, featured on the "timeline") is the remarkable strength of emotion it contains, which makes the audience not only feel sorry for Dido in her lovelorn state but also admire the nobility of her spirit and the magnanimity of her grief. The Lament is cast over a bass line that, in the repetition of its depressed descending line and rich

DRAMATIS PERSONAE

Dido Queen of Carthage . . . . soprano
Belinda her confidante . . . . soprano
Aeneas a Trojan prince . . . . baritone
Sorceress . . . . mezzo-soprano
Spirit in the form of Mercury . . . . alto/mezzo-soprano
Sailor . . . . soprano

Choruses of courtiers, witches, sailors and cupids

Setting Dido's palace at Carthage; a nearby cave; a grove; and the harbour

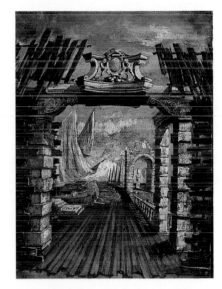

A set design for a production of *Dido and Aeneas* at Glyndebourne, England.

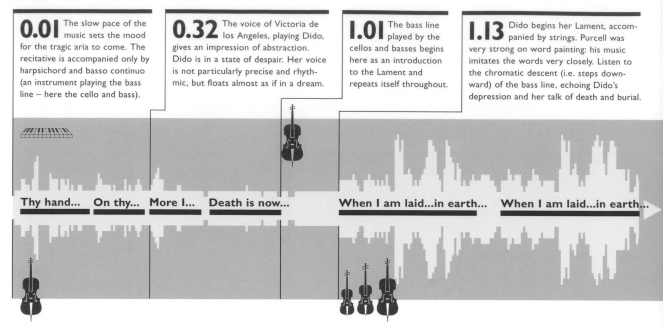

0.01 The slow pace of the music sets the mood for the tragic aria to come. The recitative is accompanied only by harpsichord and basso continuo (an instrument playing the bass line – here the cello and bass).

0.32 The voice of Victoria de los Angeles, playing Dido, gives an impression of abstraction. Dido is in a state of despair. Her voice is not particularly precise and rhythmic, but floats almost as if in a dream.

1.01 The bass line played by the cellos and basses begins here as an introduction to the Lament and repeats itself throughout.

1.13 Dido begins her Lament, accompanied by strings. Purcell was very strong on word painting: his music imitates the words very closely. Listen to the chromatic descent (i.e. steps downward) of the bass line, echoing Dido's depression and her talk of death and burial.

Thy hand... | On thy... | More I... | Death is now... | When I am laid...in earth... | When I am laid...in earth...

■ Dido

Thy hand, Belinda; darkness shades me,
On thy bosom let me rest.
More I would, but Death invades me;
Death is now a welcome guest.

[The Lament]
When I am laid in earth,
May my wrongs create no trouble
in thy breast,
Remember me, remember me,
But ah! forget my fate.

Dido impales herself before jumping on to her funeral pyre as Aeneas's Trojan fleet sets sail.

chromatic chords, musically sums up the nature of Dido's despair. The Lament acts as the emotional focus of the opera, and the poignant line "Remember me, remember me" is unforgettable. Although there is nothing else in *Dido and Aeneas* as passionate as this, all the music is of an elevated calibre. Among the other highlights are the opening (**CD track 29**), the famous Triumphal Dance and the Furies' Echo Dance in Act I and The Sailors' Dance and Witches Dance in Act III, as well as many attractive songs with memorable, even catchy tunes. The score is particularly notable for the genius of Purcell's word setting.

The libretto and its origins

The Latin poet Publius Vergilius Maro (better known as Virgil) is most famous for his epic poem *The Aeneid*, which chronicles the adventures of Aeneas and his founding of the great city of Rome. The part describing Aeneas's visit to Carthage and his ill-fated love affair with Queen Dido has captured the imagination of many composers. Among the operas with this theme, those by Purcell, Pietro Cavalli and Hector Berlioz (*Les Troyens*) are by far the best known today. Nahum Tate, the librettist of Purcell's opera, based his text on a five-act play he had originally written in 1678. An Irish librettist and playwright,

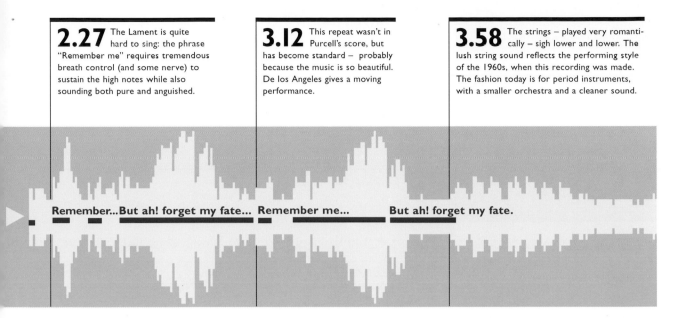

2.27 The Lament is quite hard to sing: the phrase "Remember me" requires tremendous breath control (and some nerve) to sustain the high notes while also sounding both pure and anguished.

3.12 This repeat wasn't in Purcell's score, but has become standard – probably because the music is so beautiful. De los Angeles gives a moving performance.

3.58 The strings – played very romantically – sigh lower and lower. The lush string sound reflects the performing style of the 1960s, when this recording was made. The fashion today is for period instruments, with a smaller orchestra and a cleaner sound.

Remember...But ah! forget my fate... Remember me... But ah! forget my fate.

Tate became Poet Laureate to the English court on the death of Thomas Shadwell in 1692. He was a political writer and it has been suggested that his libretto to Dido and Aeneas had a political subtext, but its precise meaning has been lost.

The composer: Henry Purcell (1659–95)

Not only was Purcell's life short but nothing has survived by way of personal testimony or recollection of his nature. What little *is* known about him comes from official records and state papers relating to his work as composer-in-ordinary (salaried composer) for the King's Violins, co organist of the Chapel Royal and organist at Westminster Abbey, where he succeeded his teacher John Blow in 1678. Even his date of birth has been derived only from evidence on his memorial in Westminster Abbey (which states that he died in his thirty-seventh year in 1695). His music is perhaps more versatile and wide-ranging than that of any other composer of his time. His legacies range from chamber music (the beautiful string fantasias), solo songs (both bawdy and sublime), music for state occasions, anthems for the Church and a huge range of incidental and operatic music for the theatre. To his friend, Thomas Tudway, Purcell was "confessedly the greatest Genius we ever had," a warm sentiment that is still echoed among music-lovers today.

The finest contemporary portrait of Purcell, by Sir Godfrey Kneller.

Above A scene from *The Beggar's Opera*, painted by William Hogarth, *c.* 1731. The opera continues the bawdy tradition of many of Purcell's songs.

Where to go next

Anyone enthusiastic about *Dido and Aeneas* who would like to find a similar style of music should start with Purcell's other operas (*see below*). Although their form differs from *Dido and Aeneas*, they are nonetheless musically very appealing. Another work with an atmosphere similar to *Dido's* is *The Beggar's Opera* (1728), first performed a generation after Purcell's death. Conceived by the poet and librettist, John Gay, it consists of a collection of tunes that were popular in England at the beginning of the eighteenth century, incorporating three airs by Purcell and many more by George Frideric Handel, Jeremiah Clarke, Giovanni Bononcini, plus popular French, Irish, Scottish and English ballads of the period. John Blow's *Venus and Adonis* of 1685, the work on which *Dido and Aeneas* was undoubtedly based, provides an enlightening background to the genre of English opera at this time.

Other operas by Purcell

Dido and Aeneas is Purcell's only true opera. The four operas listed below are semi-operas.

DIOCLESIAN

Semi-opera in five acts
Libretto by **Thomas Betterton** *adapted from* **Philip Massinger** *and* **John Fletcher's** *tragicomedy,* **The Prophetess**
Original language **English**
First performed in **London, 1690**
Approximate length **110 minutes**

Purcell's first major work for the stage is seldom performed today, although the music for Dioclesian's coronation, the defeat of the Persian army in Act IV and the long masque of Act V are very fine indeed. The story follows the life of the Roman Emperor Dioclesian from his humble boar-slaying origins as a common soldier to his lofty retirement and his admiration for the attractive Princess Aurelia.

KING ARTHUR

Semi-opera in five acts
Libretto by **John Dryden**
Original language **English**
First performed in **London, 1691**
Approximate length **180 minutes**

A spectacular semi-opera incorporating the play by English poet John Dryden about the battle between King Arthur of the Britons and King Oswald of Kent for the hand of the fair Emmeline. In the end Arthur wins, mercifully sparing Oswald's life. Although none of the principal characters has a singing role, sections of music up to thirty minutes long interrupt the play. The music, which includes the shivering song of the "Cold Genius" and the beautiful "Fairest Isle," provides many marvellous examples of the glory of Purcell's art.

Below Arthur, played by Howard Ward, leads the Britons into battle in a production of *King Arthur* at Châtelet in Paris.

THE FAIRY QUEEN

Semi-opera in five acts

Libretto **Anonymous** *after Shakespeare's*

A Midsummer Night's Dream

Original language **English**

First performed in **London, 1692**

Approximate length **130 minutes**

Shakespeare's abridged and adapted play should be the main focus of this entertainment, with Purcell's masques acting simply as enjoyable musical diversions from the main plot. As with all semi-operas of this type, the music on its own makes no dramatic sense, for it consists not of expressive arias for principal characters but of songs and dances for shepherds, peasants, gods and fairies. Modern performances often drop the play altogether, however, and perform just the music, which is a great pity. Purcell's music deals with Titania's enchanted love for Bottom and the dispute between Titania and Oberon over the Indian boy, and includes bawdy songs for drunkards and a curious finale in a Chinese Garden of Eden.

THE INDIAN QUEEN

Semi-opera in five acts (Act V by Purcell's brother, Daniel Purcell)

Libretto by **John Dryden** *and* **Robert Howard**

Original language **English**

First performed in **London, 1695**

Approximate length **180 minutes**

Unfinished at the time of the composer's death, Purcell's last major work includes the magnificent trumpet symphony "Come Ye Sons of Art Away." The story concerns the Mexican Queen, Zempoalla, in her struggles against the Incas. She is helped in part by the mercenary Inca soldier, Montezuma, who has been forced to flee his home country because of his love for the Inca princess, Horatia. Due to financial constraints the premiere of *The Indian Queen* at London's Drury Lane was not nearly as lavish as Purcell's previous productions had been.

MOZART:
DON GIOVANNI

CD tracks 30 (timeline) and 31

Opera in *two acts*
Music by *Wolfgang Amadeus Mozart*
Libretto by *Lorenzo Da Ponte*
Original language *Italian*
First performed in *Prague, 1787*
Approximate length *165 minutes*

The subtle mixture of comedy and tragedy, the acute characterization of the principal characters (who are by turns laughable and sympathetic) and the sheer vivacity of Mozart's forceful and brooding operatic score combine to make this one of the most popular and exciting operas of the entire repertoire. Perhaps the most intriguing aspect of all is the compelling portrait of Don Giovanni himself. Until recently he had been drawn as a rake, a devilish but attractive free spirit, weak of course, but ultimately heroic in his final minutes of defiance. In the modern world, however, where sexual harassment of any nature is considered singularly unfunny, modern directors have tended to paint Giovanni as an all-evil rapist and murderer, turning even his last display of bravura into cowardice. This interpretation seems to work particularly well when performed live in the opera house, and is amply backed up by the music.

A set design for Act II of *Don Giovanni*, showing the statue of the Commendatore.

Summary of the plot

Don Giovanni is pursued by Donna Anna, the young girl he has attempted to rape and whose father, the Commendatore, he has recklessly killed. He is also wanted by Donna Elvira, a lover he has forsaken, but his servant Leporello reveals to her in the famous "Catalogue song" that Giovanni has had thousands of lovers all over the world and that she means nothing to him. In an act of atrocious sexual self-confidence, Giovanni even attempts to seduce Zerlina, the bride at a peasant wedding. As the forces of disapproval amass against him, he takes shelter in a graveyard where a statue of the Commendatore tells him that he will be silenced before morning. In response Giovanni bluffingly invites the statue to dinner. That evening the statue does indeed appear at Giovanni's house, demanding that the young nobleman repent his sins. Giovanni refuses and is swallowed up, screaming, by the flames of Hell. The final moral, sung by the remaining principals, is that sinners get whatever punishment they deserve.

A brief history of the opera

Many poems, operas and ballets have been written about the fictional Spanish libertine, Don Juan, but his first appearance was in 1630 in a play called *El Burlador de Sevilla* by the monk Tirso de Molina. At least two other operas on this subject were written just before Mozart's version of 1787. As the basis for his libretto, Lorenzo Da Ponte used text by Giovanni Bertati for Giuseppe Gazzaniga's short opera, *Don Giovanni Tenorio*, which had received a successful premiere in Venice earlier in the year. Mozart's version was premiered in Prague in October 1787 where he had also enjoyed considerable success with *Le nozze di Figaro* only nine months earlier. The composer was loudly cheered and the opera, with some changes here and there to suit the demands of individual singers, has remained in the popular repertory ever since.

DRAMATIS PERSONAE

Don Giovanni a young nobleman . . . . baritone
Commendatore Donna Anna's father . . . . . bass
Donna Anna betrothed to Don Ottavio . . . soprano
Don Ottavio . . . . tenor
Donna Elvira a lady from Burgos . . . . soprano
Leporello Giovanni's servant . . . . bass
Masetto a peasant, betrothed to Zerlina . . . .bass
Zerlina a peasant girl . . . . soprano

Choruses of peasants, servants, demons and musicians

Setting A Spanish town (traditionally Seville), in the sixteenth century

Don Giovanni, played by the baritone Olaf Baer, as he is engulfed by flames at the close of the opera in a 1991 production at Glyndebourne, England.

"Là ci darem" and other highlights

"Là ci darem" (**CD track 30**: see also the "timeline") is a touching duet, remarkable primarily for the sweetness of its tone and the simplicity of

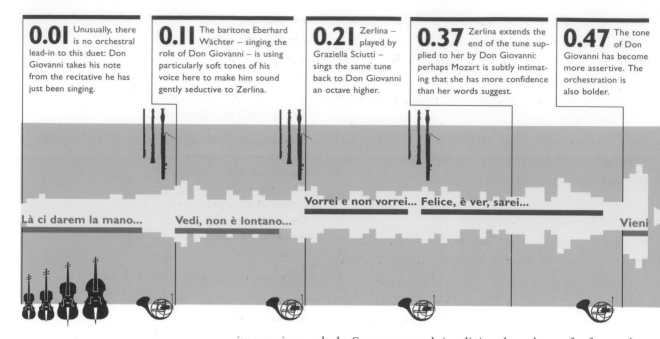

0.01 Unusually, there is no orchestral lead-in to this duet: Don Giovanni takes his note from the recitative he has just been singing.

0.11 The baritone Eberhard Wächter – singing the role of Don Giovanni – is using particularly soft tones of his voice here to make him sound gently seductive to Zerlina.

0.21 Zerlina – played by Graziella Sciutti – sings the same tune back to Don Giovanni an octave higher.

0.37 Zerlina extends the end of the tune supplied to her by Don Giovanni: perhaps Mozart is subtly intimating that she has more confidence than her words suggest.

0.47 The tone of Don Giovanni has become more assertive. The orchestration is also bolder.

Là ci darem la mano...   Vedi, non è lontano...   Vorrei e non vorrei... Felice, è ver, sarei...   Vieni

Below Don Giovanni and Zerlina singing the duet "Là ci darem la mano" in an illustration of c. 1812. *Bottom* Peter Coleman-Wright and Penelope Brister singing the same duet at the Australian Opera.

its opening melody. Sweetness and simplicity, though, are far from what really lies beneath the surface of this song. Don Giovanni is here seducing a peasant girl on her wedding day and the bride – Zerlina – is sorely tempted to follow him and forget all about her nuptial promises to the young Masetto. The satanic intention that lies behind this enchanting music, and Zerlina's frightened wavering and final acceptance of Giovanni's offer, make this one of the highlights of the opera.

The "Catalogue song" (**CD track 31**) in which Leporello introduces Don Giovanni by listing all his master's sexual conquests, and Giovanni's touching serenade to Elvira accompanied on the mandolin, are special treats. So too is the dramatic conclusion to Giovanni's party at the end of Act I and the terrifying entrance of the Commendatore, accompanied by the lugubrious tones of three trombones, in the finale of Act II. Mozart's visionary, haunting music at this moment echoes the overture, and foreshadows the dawn of the Romantic movement at the beginning of the nineteenth century.

The librettist: Lorenzo Da Ponte

Born Emmanuele Conegliano in 1749, Lorenzo Da Ponte wrote the librettos

0.51 The way Zerlina's melodic line wavers and flutters, together with the turn on the strings as she ends, indicate that her resolve is beginning to weaken.

1.01 Mozart has reflected Zerlina's attempts to resist Don Giovanni in the music: as she keeps repeating herself so too does the tune she sings, with neither the words nor the music quite coming to the point.

1.15 Don Giovanni returns to his original theme, this time doubled by a flute. Mozart may have used this high instrument to imitate Zerlina, musically suggesting that the two characters are moving together.

1.20 Zerlina is accompanied by a bassoon, perhaps echoing Don Giovanni.

mio...

Mi fà pietà...

Io cangierò tua sorte

Presto non son più forte

Vieni... Là ci darem...

Vorrei e non vorrei

Lá mi dirai... Partiam...

Mi trema...

■ **Giovanni**
Là ci darem la mano,
Là mi dirai di sì.
Vedi, non è lontano,
Partiam, ben mio, da quì.

There you will give me your hand.
There you will tell me yes.
You see it is not far.
Let us leave my beloved.

■ **Zerlina**
Vorrei e non vorrei,
Mi trema un poco il cor.
Felice, è ver, sarei,
Ma può burlarmi ancor.

I would like to, but yet I would not,
My heart trembles a little
It's true I would be happy,
But maybe he is only tricking me.

■ **Giovanni**
Vieni, mio bel diletto!

Come, my lovely girl!

■ **Zerlina**
Mi fà pietà Masetto.

I feel sorry for Masetto.

■ **Giovanni**
Io cangierò tua sorte.

I will change your life.

■ **Zerlina**
Presto non son più forte.

Soon I'll no longer be able to resist.

The Tyl Theatre in Prague, where *Don Giovanni* was first performed in 1787.

for three of the most popular operas ever written (*Don Giovanni*, *Le nozze di Figaro* and *Così fan tutte*), all by Mozart. In fact the librettist never rated Mozart as highly as he did other composers with whom he collaborated, notably Antonio Salieri and Vicente Martín y Soler. Da Ponte was so involved in scandal and intrigue that he was forced

1.44 Instead of singing in turn, Zerlina and Don Giovanni sing simultaneously for the first time. The interaction between them becomes faster and faster.

1.49 The melodic line descends, indicating Zerlina's crumbling resolve.

2.06 The turning point, as Zerlina succumbs, is very poignant musically: listen to the way Sciutti sings it with a small voice. It is followed by a very brief pause so that the audience can fully grasp what has happened.

2.12 The union of the two characters is brilliantly symbolized by their singing the same words and tune in unison.

Ma può...

Vieni... Io cangierò...

Presto non son più forte

Andiam!...

Andiam!

Andiam, andiam...

Andiam, andiam...

Ruggiero Raimondi playing Don Giovanni in the internationally acclaimed film version of the opera directed by Joseph Losey (1979).

■ **Zerlina**
Ma può burlarmi ancor.

But maybe he is only tricking me.

■ **Giovanni**
Vieni, mio bel diletto!

Come, my lovely girl!

■ **Zerlina**
Mi fà pietà Masetto.

I feel sorry for Masetto.

■ **Giovanni**
Io cangierò tua sorte.

I will change your life.

■ **Zerlina**
Presto non son più forte.

Soon I'll no longer be able to resist.

■ **Giovanni**
Andiam!

Let us go!

■ **Zerlina**
Andiam!

Let us go!

■■ **Giovanni, Zerlina**
Andiam, andiam, mio bene,
A ristorar le pene
D'un innocente amor.

Let us go, let us go, my beloved,
To soothe the pangs
Of an innocent love.

into exile. First he worked as an impresario for a theatre in London, but following his bankruptcy in 1805, he moved to the United States where he set up as a grocer and general merchant in New York, Pennsylvania and Philadelphia. He spent the rest of his life – he died in 1838 – promoting Italian food, culture and language in New York.

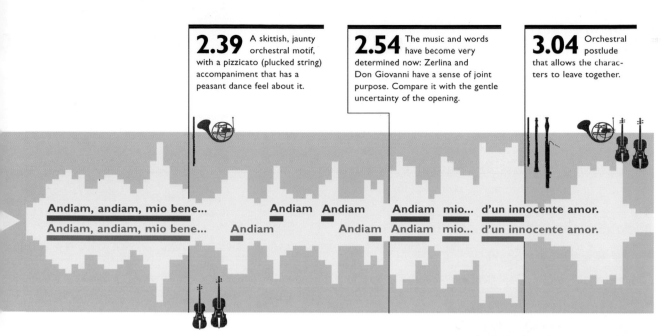

2.39 A skittish, jaunty orchestral motif, with a pizzicato (plucked string) accompaniment that has a peasant dance feel about it.

2.54 The music and words have become very determined now: Zerlina and Don Giovanni have a sense of joint purpose. Compare it with the gentle uncertainty of the opening.

3.04 Orchestral postlude that allows the characters to leave together.

Andiam, andiam, mio bene...   Andiam Andiam   Andiam mio... d'un innocente amor.
Andiam, andiam, mio bene... Andiam   Andiam Andiam mio... d'un innocente amor.

The composer: Wolfgang Amadeus Mozart (1756–91)

Many connoisseurs believe Mozart to have been the greatest composer that ever lived. Mozart was certainly the supreme exponent of the Classical style, which is characterized by beauty, elegance, purity and perfection of form. His life was short and not altogether happy. His childhood was dominated by the stifling figure of his father, who made a small fortune touring his precocious son around the courts of Europe in the early days and was reluctant to release him from his grip. Maybe Mozart never really escaped from his father's influence until the older man died, but he did manage to leave Salzburg, the home town he so much hated, and set himself up as a respected composer in Vienna. However talented Mozart was, and was perceived to be in his own lifetime, he never attained any of the better positions as composer to the nobility or to the Church. Although he worked hard, and his output of over six hundred works is certainly prodigious for his time, he always found himself in debt. After losing a court case to a wealthy patron, and following a bout of rheumatic fever, he died, still in his thirties, with his *Requiem* lying unfinished on his desk. He was buried in an unmarked pauper's grave. The composer Franz Schubert was among the pallbearers. Of all Mozart's magnificent achievements his operas are arguably the finest.

Wolfgang Amadeus Mozart, aged about thirty, shortly before he composed *Don Giovanni*.

Where to go next

There are only two other operas by Mozart that are remotely similar to *Don Giovanni* in terms of musical style, though they are both less brooding and haunted: *Le nozze di Figaro* and *Così fan tutte*. Both with librettos by Da Ponte, they are considered the peak of Mozart's operatic achievement, and many would hold that they are the most sophisticated and subtle works of music theatre ever composed. For the sake of interest it is well worth getting to know the one-act *Don Giovanni Tenorio* by Giuseppe Gazzaniga, composed just a year before Mozart's version. Though seldom performed, it has been recorded many times and contains some fine musical moments.

Above Kiri Te Kanawa as the Countess in Mozart's *Le nozze di Figaro*.

Other operas by Mozart

Despite his short life, Mozart wrote many operas, all very different from each other in character and binding musical form. Common to all of them, though, is an astute sense of musical characterization that was quite unique for its time. His most popular operas are discussed below.

IDOMENEO (Idomeneus, King of Crete)

Opera in three acts
Libretto by Giovanni Varesco after Antoine Danchet's
libretto for Campra's opera, **Idomenée**
Original language Italian
First performed in Munich, 1781
Approximate length 220 minutes

In Mozart's first mature opera, Idomeneo, the king of Crete during the Trojan War, pledges to sacrifice the first living creature he sees if Neptune will allow him a safe sea crossing from Troy. When that creature turns out to be his son, Idamante, the king unsurprisingly reneges on his promise. A vicious sea monster comes to persecute the islanders but is killed by Idamante, who then offers himself as a sacrifice. Luckily Neptune intervenes to save the day. Idomeneo abdicates so that Idamante and his young bride, Ilia, can assume the throne. The music is both dignified and heroic.

DIE ENTFUHRUNG AUS DEM SERAIL (The Abduction from the Seraglio)

Opera in three acts
Libretto by Gottlieb Stephanie after Friedrich Bretzner's
libretto for André's opera, **Belmont und Konstanze**
Original language German
First performed in Vienna, 1782
Approximate length 135 minutes

Mozart's comic German opera was an instant success and contains some of Mozart's most imaginative and delightful music. The plot is set in Turkey where Pasha Selim and his harem-keeper, the ridiculous Osmin, are holding captive against their wills Konstanze, a noble Spanish lady, and her maid. Konstanze's betrothed, Belmonte, plans their escape but the plot is foiled. Due to a series of unlikely circumstances, the Pasha eventually agrees to release them anyway. On first hearing this work the Holy Roman Emperor Joseph II was reputed to have said: "Too many notes, my dear Mozart."

Below A scene from a Metropolitan Opera production of *Idomeneo* in New York; the spectacular set features the head of Neptune, God of the Sea, at the back of the stage.

LE NOZZE DI FIGARO (The Marriage of Figaro)

Opera in four acts
Libretto by **Lorenzo Da Ponte** *after Beaumarchais' play,*
La Folle Journée ou Le Mariage de Figaro
Original language **Italian**
First performed in **Vienna, 1786**
Approximate length **180 minutes**

Mozart's brilliant and enduring farce was the first of his three collaborations with Da Ponte. Figaro, hoping to marry the maid Susanna, has to stop his licentious master, the Count, from having his way with her first. The Countess joins Figaro and Susanna in plots to expose and humiliate the Count while the amorous dalliances of the pageboy, Cherubino, who seems to lust after every female in the story, serve only to fuel the Count's rage. Mozart's warm-hearted musical characterizations bring richness and profundity to an otherwise frivolous scenario.

COSÌ FAN TUTTE (Women are all the same)

Opera in two acts
Libretto by **Lorenzo Da Ponte**
Original language **Italian**
First performed in **Vienna, 1790**
Approximate length **180 minutes**

Two young men, Guglielmo and Ferrando, wager Don Alfonso that if they were to go away their girlfriends would remain faithful. They pretend to have been called up for military service but reappear disguised as Albanians and attempt to seduce each other's girlfriends. The girls turn out to be fickle indeed. Despite this empty plot the opera contains some of Mozart's most beautiful and serene music.

DIE ZAUBERFLOTE (The Magic Flute)

Opera in two acts
Libretto by **Emanuel Schikaneder** *partly after*
Abbé Jean Terrasson's Sethos *and* **Weiland's** *fairy tale,*
Lulu from Oschinnstan
Original language **German**
First performed in **Vienna, 1791**
Approximate length **150 minutes**

In a strange fairy-tale plot, partly influenced by Mozart's involvement with a Viennese order of Freemasons, Tamino is asked by the Queen of the Night to rescue her daughter Pamina from Sarastro, the mysterious priest of a religious sect. As it turns out Sarastro is good, while the Queen of the Night has evil intentions. Tamino is united with Pamina after a ritual induction involving fire, water and the magic flute. The flapping antics of Papageno, the bird catcher, bring added mirth to the story.

LA CLEMENZA DI TITO (The Clemency of Titus)

Opera in two acts
Libretto by **Caterino Mazzolà** *after the*
drama by **Pietro Metastasio**
Original language **Italian**
First performed in **Prague, 1791**
Approximate length **135 minutes**

Commissioned for an *opera seria* in the old style, Mozart wrote his last opera in only eighteen days. In fact he was ill and still busy on *Die Zauberflöte*, so he found no pleasure in writing *Tito*. Although not Mozart's finest work, it is nonetheless unjustly neglected. The plot concludes with the Emperor Titus's magnanimous gesture of forgiveness to all those who plotted but failed to murder him.

Left Trevor Nunn's staging of *Così fan tutte*, produced at the Glyndebourne Festival in England.

ROSSINI:
IL BARBIERE
DI SIVIGLIA

CD tracks 32 (timeline) and 33

(The Barber of Seville)
Opera in *two acts*
Music by *Gioacchino Rossini*
Libretto by *Cesare Sterbini* after *Pierre Augustin Caron de Beaumarchais' play,* Le Barbier de Séville
Original language *Italian*
First performed in *Rome, 1816*
Approximate length *130 minutes*

Rolando Panerai (Figaro) shaves Fernando Corena (Doctor Bartolo) in an attempt to distract him from the activities of the two young lovers, Rosina and Almaviva, in Act II.

Opera houses all over the world know that any season will be financially subsidized by a run of Rossini's *Il barbiere di Siviglia*. As a purely comic opera its success is unparalleled. The combination of Rossini's light and vivacious music, so perfectly suited to comic subjects, with Beaumarchais' hilariously farcical plot, makes for a frothy and ebullient evening out that continues to delight audiences of millions every year. *Il barbiere* is not a highbrow opera but sheer entertainment in a most enjoyable and frivolous form.

Summary of the plot

Rosina is kept locked away by her jealous guardian, Doctor Bartolo, who has designs on her inheritance and is afraid that she might fall in love with some young man and leave him. To gain access to the doctor's house, Rosina's dashing suitor, the Count Almaviva, disguises himself first as a drunken soldier and then as "Don Alonso," a young priest standing in for Rosina's singing teacher, Don Basilio. When the real Don Basilio arrives he is sent packing with a bribe by the Count. Almaviva eventually succeeds – with the artful help of his cunning aid, Figaro (the barber of Seville) – in marrying Rosina by extracting a marriage contract from a notary whose intention was originally to marry Rosina to her hated guardian, Bartolo.

A brief history of the opera

The opera was first entitled *Almaviva, o L'inutile precauzione* (Almaviva, or the Useless Precaution) to distinguish it from the highly successful *Il barbiere di Siviglia* (1782) by the prolific composer Giovanni Paisiello. Rossini was rushed off his feet as usual, and the score had to be prepared for the Rome Carnival season of 1816 in little over two weeks. The famous overture was adapted from the overture to his earlier opera, *Aureliano in Palmira* of 1813 (and was recycled again for *Elisabetta, Regina d'Inghilterra*, 1815); contrary to popular belief, it is not a deliberate attempt to parody the sounds of Spanish music. The Roman premiere was not well received probably because of the haste of the preparations. It did not take long, however, for the wit and delightful originality of Rossini's score to capture the imagination of a wide and enthusiastic public and to prompt Rossini to change its name back to *Il barbiere di Siviglia* without fear of unfavourable comparison with Paisiello's opera.

"Largo al factotum" and other highlights

Figaro's arietta "Largo al factotum" (Make way for the factotum: CD **track 32**, featured on the "timeline") is the most famous song from this opera and is a quintessential example of Rossini's comic touch at its best. This is Figaro's first song, in which he introduces himself to the audience. He boasts that he is "a barber of quality," much needed by everyone in the town. He congratulates himself on the pleasures of his life and rattles off an account of his daily tasks and the many demands made of him in words that get faster and faster until he is left to sing unaccompanied "Figaro, Figaro, Figaro, Figaro..." – a real test of vocal agility for the baritone voice. The opera is also notable for the

DRAMATIS PERSONAE

Count Almaviva . . . . tenor
Doctor Bartolo a physician
and Rosina's guardian . . . . bass/baritone
Rosina wealthy heiress . . . . mezzo-soprano
Figaro a barber . . . . baritone
Don Basilio a music teacher
and hypocrite . . . . bass
Florello Count Almaviva's servant . . . bass
Ambrogio Bartolo's servant . . . . bass
Berta Bartolo's housekeeper . . . . mezzo-soprano
Officer . . . . baritone
Notary . . . . silent

Choruses of musicians, soldiers, police officers

Setting Seville in the eighteenth century

A costume design for Figaro, the barber, for a 1905 production of the opera.

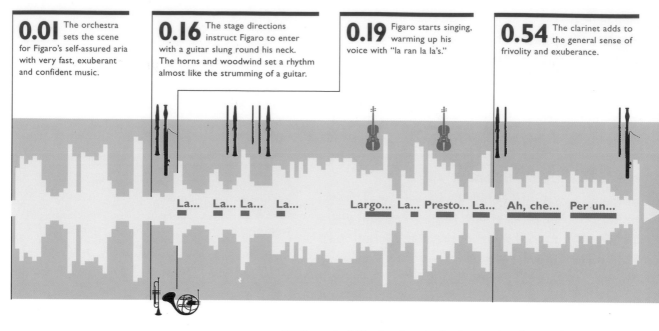

0.01 The orchestra sets the scene for Figaro's self-assured aria with very fast, exuberant and confident music.

0.16 The stage directions instruct Figaro to enter with a guitar slung round his neck. The horns and woodwind set a rhythm almost like the strumming of a guitar.

0.19 Figaro starts singing, warming up his voice with "la ran la la's."

0.54 The clarinet adds to the general sense of frivolity and exuberance.

La... La... La... La...   Largo... La... Presto... La...   Ah, che... Per un...

overture (**CD track 33**); the frantic finales to the first and second acts; Almaviva's beautiful serenade to Rosina, "Ecco ridente in cielo," at the beginning of Act I; and for the many examples of Rossini's florid, technically dazzling solos for the mezzo-soprano voice of Rosina.

A nineteenth-century painting of a street scene in Seville, where Rossini set his most popular opera.

The libretto and librettist

Although Cesare Sterbini (1784–1831) was an official of the Vatican Treasury, a poet and a fluent Latin-, Greek-, French- and German-speaker, he still found time to write librettos for operas. His first collaboration with Rossini, *Torvaldo e Dorliska*, was a clumsy mess. Rossini nevertheless asked Sterbini to provide the text for *Il barbiere*, which turned out to be his only lasting success as a librettist. The story was based on a play by Pierre Augustin Caron de Beaumarchais, *Le Barbier de Séville*, the first of a trilogy of plays. Rossini and Sterbini were not the first to recognize the comic operatic potential *Le Barbier*: at least three other composers had already written operas on the same theme (F.L. Benda, Giovanni Paisiello and Nicolas Isouard). The second part of the trilogy, *Le Mariage de Figaro*, which was made especially famous by Mozart's opera, is still popular

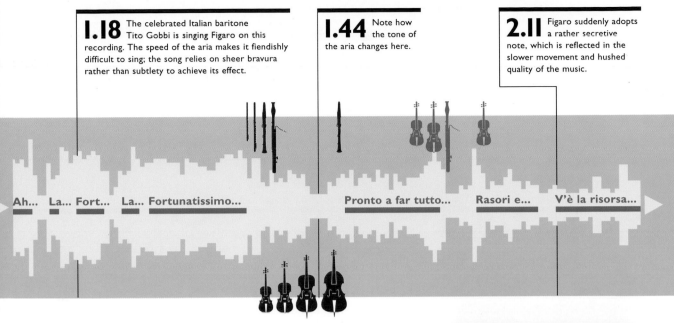

1.18 The celebrated Italian baritone Tito Gobbi is singing Figaro on this recording. The speed of the aria makes it fiendishly difficult to sing; the song relies on sheer bravura rather than subtlety to achieve its effect.

1.44 Note how the tone of the aria changes here.

2.11 Figaro suddenly adopts a rather secretive note, which is reflected in the slower movement and hushed quality of the music.

Ah... La... Fort... La... Fortunatissimo... Pronto a far tutto... Rasori e... V'è la risorsa...

■ **Figaro**

La ran la lera, la ran la la!	La ran la lera, la ran la la!
Largo al factotum della città!	Make way for the factotum of the city
La ran la, la ran la, la ran la la!	La ran la, la ran la, la ran la la!
Presto a bottega	Rushing to his shop
che l'alba è già.	as dawn is here,
La ran la, la ran la, la ran la la!	La ran la, la ran la, la ran la la!
Ah, che bel vivere,	What a fine life,
che bel piacere,	what merry pleasures
Per un barbiere di qualità.	For a barber of quality.
Ah, bravo Figaro,	Ah, bravo Figaro,
Bravo, bravissimo, bravo!	Bravo, bravissimo, bravo!
La ran la, la ran la, la ran la la!	La ran la, la ran la, la ran la la!
Fortunatissimo,	Luckiest of men,
per verità. Bravo!	indeed you are! Bravo!
La ran la, la ran la, la ran la la!	La ran la, la ran la, la ran la la!
Pronto a far tutto,	Ready for everything,
la notte, il giorno,	night or day,
Sempre d'intorno,	Always on the move,
in giro sta.	running about,
Miglior cuccagna	A better lot
per un barbiere,	for a barber,
Vita più nobile, no, non si dà.	A nobler life cannot exist.
La ran la, la ran la, la ran la la!	La ran la, la ran la, la ran la la!
Rasori e pettini, lancette e forbici,	Razors and combs, lancets and scissors,
Al mio comando tutto qui sta.	At my command, everything's ready.
V'è la risorsa,	Then there's the extras,
poi del mestiere,	part of my trade,
Colla donnetta, col cavaliere...	Business for ladies, and gentlemen...

The French baritone François Le Roux playing Figaro, the barber of Seville.

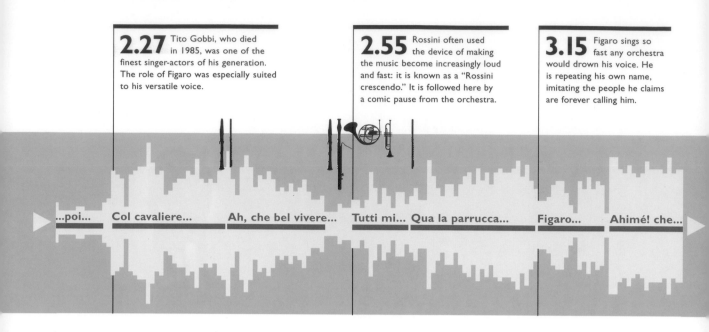

2.27 Tito Gobbi, who died in 1985, was one of the finest singer-actors of his generation. The role of Figaro was especially suited to his versatile voice.

2.55 Rossini often used the device of making the music become increasingly loud and fast: it is known as a "Rossini crescendo." It is followed here by a comic pause from the orchestra.

3.15 Figaro sings so fast any orchestra would drown his voice. He is repeating his own name, imitating the people he claims are forever calling him.

...poi... | Col cavaliere... | Ah, che bel vivere... | Tutti mi... | Qua la parrucca... | Figaro... | Ahimé! che...

A caricature of Rossini from 1867, depicting the composer as a noisy and larger-than-life character.

Col cavaliere, tra la la la.
Ah, che bel vivere, che bel piacere,
Per un barbiere di qualità.
Tutti mi chiedono, tutti mi vogliono,
Donne, ragazzi, vecchi, fanciulle.
Qua la parrucca, presto la barba,
Qua la sanguigna,
Presto il biglietto.
Figaro! Figaro! Figaro...
Ahimè! che furia! Ahimè! che folla!
Uno alla volta, per carità!
Ehi Figaro! Son qua!
Figaro qua, Figaro là,
Figaro su, Figaro giù.
Pronto, prontissimo son come il fulmine,
Sono il factotum della città.
Ah, bravo, Figaro, bravo, bravissimo,
Fortunatissimo, per verità.
A te la fortuna non mancherà.
Sono il factotum della città.

Business for gentlemen, tra la la la.
What a fine life, what merry pleasures,
for a barber of quality.
Everyone calls me, everyone wants me,
Ladies, children, old men and maidens.
"I need a wig; I want a shave;
leeches to bleed me;
here take this note."
Ho, Figaro!
Gosh! what a furore! What a crowd!
One at a time, for heaven's sake.
Ho, Figaro, I am here!
Figaro here, Figaro there,
Figaro up, Figaro down,
Quick as can be, like a flash of lightning,
Make way for the factotum of the city.
Ah, bravo Figaro, bravo, bravissimo,
Luckiest of men, indeed you are.
Good fortune will always smile on you.
I am the factotum of the city,

in France as a play. *Tartuffe*, the last part of the trilogy, was not set to music until Darius Milhaud's now-neglected opera of 1966.

The composer: Gioacchino Rossini (1792–1868)

Gioacchino Rossini's life was noted for its merriment and success. From his second opera, *La cambiale di matrimonio* (The Marriage Contract),

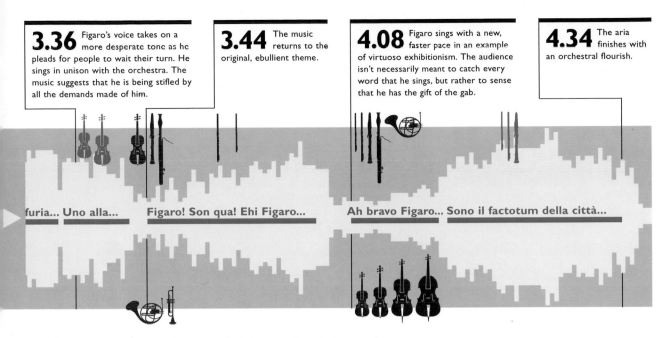

3.36 Figaro's voice takes on a more desperate tone as he pleads for people to wait their turn. He sings in unison with the orchestra. The music suggests that he is being stifled by all the demands made of him.

3.44 The music returns to the original, ebullient theme.

4.08 Figaro sings with a new, faster pace in an example of virtuoso exhibitionism. The audience isn't necessarily meant to catch every word that he sings, but rather to sense that he has the gift of the gab.

4.34 The aria finishes with an orchestral flourish.

furia... Uno alla...   Figaro! Son qua! Ehi Figaro...   Ah bravo Figaro... Sono il factotum della città...

which he composed at the age of eighteen, Rossini gained a reputation in Italy as a brilliant, sometimes dazzling composer. With the heroic melodrama *Tancredi* he achieved international success as early as 1813. In a packed life, Rossini rose from his musical background in Pesaro, central Italy (his mother was a singer, his father a horn player) to become one of the world's most influential composers. After composing almost forty operas, many of which were written during a long stay in Paris, Rossini decided to give up his illustrious career and lived nearly another forty years without composing a single opera. The

reasons for this extraordinary retirement were many. Fashion was changing and he wanted to quit while he was at the top. He was also badly affected by the death of his beloved mother, and was now a wealthy man in failing health who could devote himself entirely to his remarkable enthusiasm for good food and wine. Rossini was a noted wit and bon viveur who, in his later years, wrote many recipes (he is still remembered today for his invention of the famous "Rossini steak"). A few sacred works from his later years remain popular today, most notably the "Petite messe solennelle."

A scene from Act II of *Il barbiere di Siviglia* at the Royal Opera House in London.

Where to go next

Rossini's *buffo* (comic) style did not change substantially from his first to his last comedy. *La Cenerentola* and *L'Italiana in Algeri* are his two most popular comedies after the *Il barbiere di Siviglia* and bear many stylistic similarities. Of Gaetano Donizetti's *buffo* operas, *L'elisir d'amore* and *Don Pasquale* are by far his most successful. Both frothy and good humoured, these works are as delightful in their easy melodic invention and light orchestral accompaniment as Rossini's *Il barbiere*.

Left Geraint Evans as Dr Dulcamara in Donizetti's *L'elisir d'amore*.

Other operas by Rossini

Rossini composed some thirty-nine operas in total. Not all of these are as entertaining as *Il barbiere di Siviglia* – his tragedies in particular may seem lightweight to some modern listeners – but thanks to his comedies Rossini is justly remembered as one of the greatest operatic composers of his generation.

LA CAMBIALE DI MATRIMONIO (The Marriage Contract)

Opera in one act
Libretto by Gaetano Rossi after Camillo Federici's comedy
Original language Italian
First performed in Venice, 1810
Approximate length 80 minutes
This fizzing comedy propelled the eighteen-year-old Rossini into the limelight with only his second opera. A Canadian merchant named Slook promises Sir Tobias Mill a substantial reward if he can find him a wife. Tobias offers the merchant his own daughter, Fanny, but she is in love with another man: the handsome Edoardo. When Slook realizes how strongly the two young lovers feel about each other he offers to bequeath his inheritance to Edoardo, thereby helping them to win her father round to their marriage.

LA SCALA DI SETA (The Silken Ladder)

Opera in one act
Libretto by Giuseppe Maria Foppa after Planard's libretto to Pierre Gaveaux' **L'Echelle de Soie**
Original language Italian

First performed in Venice, 1812
Approximate length 85 minutes
Famous now for its overture more than anything else, Rossini's light-hearted farce narrates the frivolous story of Giulia and her attempts to avoid marriage to Blansac, whom her guardian had chosen as her husband. In the course of the farce, she reveals that she has already been married secretly to Dorvil. In the end she manages to find another match for Blansac (her cousin Lucilla) and her guardian finally gives his blessing to the secret marriage.

TANCREDI

Opera in two acts
Libretto by Gaetano Rossi after Voltaire's **Tancrede** *and Tasso's* **Gerusalemme liberata**
Original language Italian
First performed in Venice, 1813
Approximate length 165 minutes
A melodrama in mature style, this opera quickly established Rossini's reputation as a popular composer, and is considered his first great opera. Tancredi heroically rescues Amenaide from execution even though he believes her to be a faithless lover. The two are reunited and all plots against them thwarted. Rossini later wrote a tragic ending for a performance of the opera in Ferrara, but it was deeply unpopular with the audience.

L'ITALIANA IN ALGERI (The Italian Girl in Algiers)

Opera in two acts
Libretto by Angelo Anelli

Original language Italian
First performed in Venice, 1813
Approximate length 135 minutes

In his first full-length *opera buffa* Rossini sets to music a racy story about a girl called Isabella, searching for her lost lover Lindoro. She is shipwrecked off the coast of Algiers where the local potentate, the tyrannical Mustafa, is holding Lindoro prisoner and slave. Mustafa has tired of his own wife, Elvira, and inevitably falls for Isabella. His plan is to marry Elvira off to Lindoro and marry Isabella himself. He is tricked, however, into joining an invented religious sect, and Lindoro and Isabella manage to make their escape during Mustafa's farcical initiation ceremony. Mustafa is reunited with his wife at the end. The most frequently performed of Rossini's operas after *Il barbiere*, this work contains a fine septet at the end of Act I and many splendid comic scenes.

LA CENERENTOLA (Cinderella)

Opera in two acts
Libretto by Jacopo Ferretti after Charles Guillaume Etienne's libretto for Steibelt's opera based on Perrault's version of the Cinderella fairy tale
Original language Italian
First performed in Rome, 1817
Approximate length 150 minutes

A moving comedy based on the fairy tale of Cinderella. The prince discovers the ill-treated Angiolina when he arrives, dressed as his valet, at the house where she lives. He orchestrates a ball in order to find himself a wife and Angiolina manages to get there despite the efforts of her wicked sisters to preclude her. When the prince recognizes her bracelet, he proclaims her to be his wife – much to the amazement and fury of her odious sisters.

GUILLAUME TELL (William Tell)

Opera in four acts
Libretto by Victor Joseph Etienne de Jouy, Florent Bis and Armand Marast after Friedrich von Schiller
Original language French
First performed in Paris, 1829
Approximate length 225 minutes

Rossini's last opera, composed for the Paris opera house, is written in the true tradition of French "grand opera." Particularly famous is the gallop from the overture that was used for many years as the signature tune to the *Lone Ranger* radio series. The story concerns the Swiss hero, William Tell, and his victorious assaults against Austrian invaders. It features the notorious incident in which he shoots an apple off his son's head, and includes a fine dramatic part for the good-natured Austrian princess, Mathilde.

Left Isabella, played by Agnes Baltsa, and the chorus of eunuchs from *L'Italiana in Algeri*. **Below** Jemmy (Tell's son) is held aloft in a scene from *Guillaume Tell* at the Royal Opera House, London.

VERDI:
RIGOLETTO

CD tracks 34 (timeline) and 35

Opera in *three acts*
Music by *Giuseppe Verdi*
Libretto by *Francesco Piave* after *Victor Hugo's play,*
Le Roi s'amuse
Original language *Italian*
First performed in *Venice, 1851*
Approximate length *120 minutes*

In *Rigoletto*, the story and the music carry you along like an express train. Verdi himself was extremely proud of it; he recognized that he had succeeded in composing a more concise, more dramatically urgent and more humanly realistic opera than ever before. The music is abundantly tuneful, and yet at the same time it sustains throughout an atmosphere of sinister intrigue and unease that is wholly consistent with the plot. Key to the success of *Rigoletto* is the enigmatic character of the title-role himself. Rigoletto is a nasty, hard and uncouth hunch-back, but he manages to win the hearts of the audience because of his deep love for his daughter, Gilda. The opera's subtle balance of humour and tragedy is another reason for its success. The unprecedented popularity of *Rigoletto* brought Verdi to new heights of national and international acclaim, establishing him during his lifetime as Italy's leading composer. The opera has remained one of the best-loved works of the entire operatic repertoire ever since.

Summary of the plot
The libertine Duke of Mantua is holding a ball at his palace. While he flirts with the Countess Ceprano, his hunchbacked jester Rigoletto

Jonathan Miller's famous production of *Rigoletto* moved the action from sixteenth-century Mantua to 1950s gangland New York. The title role is played here by the baritone John Rawnsley (centre).

mocks her husband, the Count. The party is interrupted by the arrival of Count Monterone, who publicly denounces the Duke for dishonouring his daughter. Rigoletto makes fun of Monterone, who in his fury puts a curse on the jester. Later that evening, Rigoletto's beloved daughter, Gilda, is abducted by the vengeful Count Ceprano. He takes her to the palace, where she is seduced by the Duke. Rigoletto, confirmed in the belief that Monterone's curse is taking its hold, swears revenge. He hires an assassin named Sparafucile to kill the Duke. Sparafucile's sister, Maddalena, is to lure the Duke to his death. However, Rigoletto and Gilda (who believes in her innocence that the Duke genuinely loves her) overhear the Duke attempting to seduce Maddalena. Rigoletto tries to console his daughter and sends her home. Meanwhile, he arranges for Sparafucile to deliver the Duke's body at midnight. Gilda returns in disguise to overhear Maddalena pleading with her brother to spare the Duke, with whom she has now fallen in love. Sparafucile agrees as long as they can find another corpse to present to Rigoletto. Gilda resolves to sacrifice herself. When Rigoletto returns with his money at midnight he is handed a sack containing what he believes to be the Duke's body, but he hears the Duke's voice in the distance and opens the sack to discover his daughter on the point of death. Gilda comforts her grieving father before she dies. Monterone's curse is fulfilled and Rigoletto collapses in despair.

DRAMATIS PERSONAE

The Duke of Mantua . . . . tenor
Rigoletto, his hunchbacked jester . . . baritone
Gilda, Rigoletto's daughter . . . . soprano
Sparafucile, a hired assassin . . . . bass
Maddalena, Sparafucile's sister . . . . . contralto
Giovanna, Gilda's duenna . . . . soprano
Count Monterone . . . . bass/baritone
Marullo, a nobleman . . . . baritone
Borsa, a courtier . . . . tenor
Count Ceprano . . . . bass
Countess Ceprano . . . . mezzo-soprano
Court Usher . . . . bass/baritone
Page . . . . mezzo-soprano

Choruses of noblemen, ladies, pages and halberdiers

Setting In and around Mantua in the sixteenth century

A 1935 set design for the second scene in Act I, showing the street of Rigoletto's house.

A brief history of the opera

Victor Hugo's play *Le Roi s'amuse* was banned in liberal Paris after a single performance in 1832 because the censors believed it too seditious and debauched for public consumption. Verdi, however, considered the play "the greatest subject and perhaps the greatest drama of modern times," and had been toying with the idea of turning it into an opera as early as September 1849. His sketches for an opera bearing the title *La maledizione* (The Curse) were greeted with inevitable disapproval by the Italian censors, who accused Verdi of squandering his talents on "repellent immorality and obscene triviality." The opera

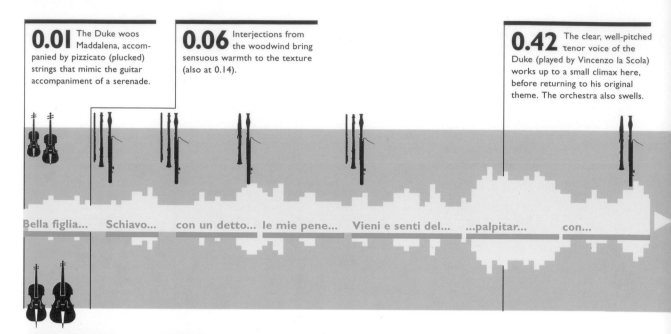

0.01 The Duke woos Maddalena, accompanied by pizzicato (plucked) strings that mimic the guitar accompaniment of a serenade.

0.06 Interjections from the woodwind bring sensuous warmth to the texture (also at 0.14).

0.42 The clear, well-pitched tenor voice of the Duke (played by Vincenzo la Scola) works up to a small climax here, before returning to his original theme. The orchestra also swells.

Bella figlia... Schiavo... con un detto... le mie pene... Vieni e senti del... ...palpitar... con...

The great Italian tenor Enrico Caruso (1873–1921) as the Duke of Mantua, which was one of his favourite roles.

■ **Duke**

Bella figlia dell'amore,
schiavo son dei vezzi tuoi;
con un detto sol tu puoi
le mie pene consolar.
Vieni e senti del mio core
il frequente palpitar.

Fairest daughter of love,
I am a slave to your charms;
just one word from you,
would soothe my every pain.
Come over here and feel
how my heart is racing.

■ **Maddalena**

Ah! Ah! rido ben di core,
chè tai baie costan poco;
quanto valga il vostro gioco,
mel credete, sò apprezzar.
Sono avvezza, bel signore,
ad un simile scherzare.

Ah! Ha! You make me laugh,
words like yours are cheap;
believe me, I know exactly
what your little game is.
I, my fine fellow, am well used
to your sort of game.

■ **Gilda**

Ah! così parlar d'amore
a me pur l'infame ho udito!
Infelice cor tradito,
per angoscia non scoppiar.

Ah! these very words of love
the scoundrel once spoke to me!
O wretched heart betrayed,
do not break for sorrow.

■ **Rigoletto**

Taci, il piangere non vale;
ch'ei mentiva sei sicura.
Taci, e mia sarà la cura
la vendetta d'affrettar.
Sì, pronta fia, sarà fatale;
io saprollo fulminar.

Hush now! tears cannot help;
now you are convinced he is a liar.
Hush now! I'll work it out,
I will hasten our revenge.
It will be quick and deadly;
I know what to do with him.

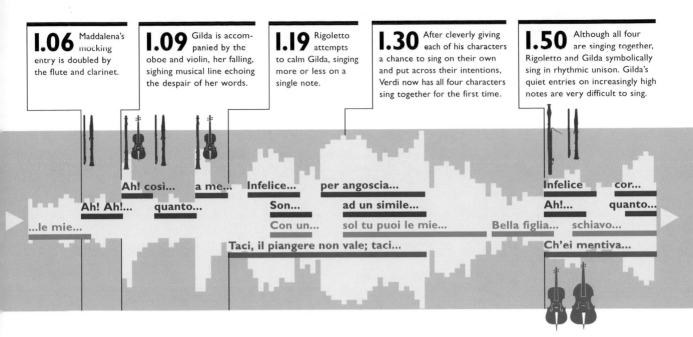

1.06 Maddalena's mocking entry is doubled by the flute and clarinet.

1.09 Gilda is accompanied by the oboe and violin, her falling, sighing musical line echoing the despair of her words.

1.19 Rigoletto attempts to calm Gilda, singing more or less on a single note.

1.30 After cleverly giving each of his characters a chance to sing on their own and put across their intentions, Verdi now has all four characters sing together for the first time.

1.50 Although all four are singing together, Rigoletto and Gilda symbolically sing in rhythmic unison. Gilda's quiet entries on increasingly high notes are very difficult to sing.

...le mie...

Ah! Ah!...

Ah! così...

quanto...

a me...

Infelice...

Son...

Con un...

per angoscia...

ad un simile...

sol tu puoi le mie...

Taci, il piangere non vale; taci...

Infelice...

Ah!...

Bella figlia...

cor...

quanto...

schiavo...

Ch'ei mentiva...

was redrafted in 1850 as *Il Duca di Vendome*, but Verdi rejected Piave's libretto for being dramatically weak. Completely overhauled and retitled *Rigoletto*, the words were at last acceptable to all parties. Verdi completed the score in forty days, in time for the first performance. The premiere – which took place at the famous Venetian Opera House, La Fenice, on 11 March 1851 – was a roaring success. News spread quickly, and within ten years *Rigoletto* had been performed at over 250 opera houses around the world.

The quartet "Bella figlia dell'amore" and other highlights

As well as being a quartet of outstanding quality and beauty, "Bella figlia dell'amore" (CD track 34: see "timeline") is also the point of greatest musical tension in the opera. It takes place in the final act, when Gilda realizes that the man she loves (the Duke) is a philandering liar and her father strengthens his resolve to take revenge on his daughter's seducer. As a duet for Rigoletto and Gilda alone it would have been powerful enough, but Verdi doubles

The title page of the original score of *Rigoletto* for voice and piano, showing the four principal characters singing the quartet, "Bella figlia dell'amore."

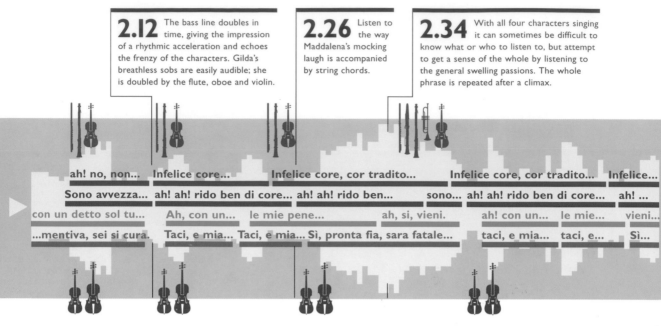

2.12 The bass line doubles in time, giving the impression of a rhythmic acceleration and echoes the frenzy of the characters. Gilda's breathless sobs are easily audible; she is doubled by the flute, oboe and violin.

2.26 Listen to the way Maddalena's mocking laugh is accompanied by string chords.

2.34 With all four characters singing it can sometimes be difficult to know what or who to listen to, but attempt to get a sense of the whole by listening to the general swelling passions. The whole phrase is repeated after a climax.

ah! no, non... Infelice core... Infelice core, cor tradito... Infelice core, cor tradito... Infelice...

Sono avvezza... ah! ah! rido ben di core... ah! ah! rido ben... sono... ah! ah! rido ben di core... ah! ...

con un detto sol tu... Ah, con un... le mie pene... ah, si, vieni. ah! con un... le mie... vieni...

...mentiva, sei si cura. Taci, e mia... Taci, e mia... Sì, pronta fia, sara fatale... taci, e mia... taci, e... Sì...

The title page from the piano version of *Rigoletto*, 1890.

the intensity by overlaying parts for the flirting Duke and the mocking Maddalena. The whole scene brims with dramatic ironies that give added impulse to the keen characterization of Verdi's music. Maddalena's music laughs and chatters while Gilda's is, by contrast, sighing and breathless. Rigoletto, with his determination for revenge, is rooted to the bass while the Duke sings in exaggerated, swaggering tones of love. What is so remarkable about the quartet is the way in which Verdi manages to combine these characterizations at one time.

Rigoletto, like *Il trovatore* and *La traviata*, the operas that immediately followed it, is extraordinarily rich in melodic invention. The tune that is best remembered, though, is the Duke's jaunty aria, "La donna è mobile" from Act III (**CD track 35**), in which the Duke justifies his bad treatment of women by describing how cunning and fickle they are. Verdi knew the song would be a hit from the start and it was soon taken up by the street musicians of his day. Gilda's only aria is "Caro nome" from Act I, which is not so much a showpiece of coloratura technique as a challenge of a singer's innate musicality as she tenderly remembers the name of her first love. At the beginning of the opera, the Duke's throwaway short, fast aria, "Questa o quella" (This girl or that), another misogynistic song, has become a favourite concert showpiece for tenors such as Luciano Pavarotti and Placido Domingo.

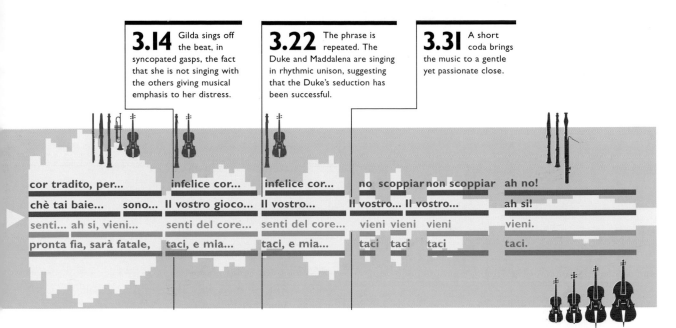

3.14 Gilda sings off the beat, in syncopated gasps, the fact that she is not singing with the others giving musical emphasis to her distress.

3.22 The phrase is repeated. The Duke and Maddalena are singing in rhythmic unison, suggesting that the Duke's seduction has been successful.

3.31 A short coda brings the music to a gentle yet passionate close.

cor tradito, per...   infelice cor...   infelice cor...   no scoppiar non scoppiar   ah no!

chè tai baie...   sono...   Il vostro gioco...   Il vostro...   Il vostro... Il vostro...   ah si!

senti... ah si, vieni...   senti del core...   senti del core...   vieni vieni vieni   vieni.

pronta fia, sarà fatale,   taci, e mia...   taci, e mia...   taci taci taci   taci.

The composer: Giuseppe Verdi (1813–1901)

The son of an innkeeper and grocer from the village of Le Roncole in Italy, Giuseppe Verdi was to become the leading Italian composer of the nineteenth century. A wealthy merchant sponsored his musical education in Milan and later became his father-in-law. When his wife and both of his children died, Verdi resolved to give up opera altogether, with only two operas behind him (one of them the failed comedy *Un giorno di regno,* A One-day Reign). He was persuaded otherwise, however, and the national success of the opera that followed, *Nabucco* (1842), launched him on a long and successful career – and also introduced him to his second wife, the singer Giuseppina Strepponi, who took part in the premiere at La Scala. Verdi collaborated with the librettist Francesco Maria Piave (1819–76) on many operas, including *Ernani, I due Foscari, Attila, Macbeth, Il corsaro, Stiffelio, Rigoletto, La traviata, Simon Boccanegra* and *La forza del destino.* Verdi and Piave had a tense though long-lasting friendship, and Piave allowed Verdi to make endless changes to his libretti. Interestingly, Piave's libretti for other composers were never as polished as those he wrote for Verdi. When Giuseppina died in 1897, Verdi's health also went into decline. He died of a stroke at his home in Milan on 27 January 1901, causing the Italian nation to go into mourning.

Giuseppe Verdi was so distraught by the death of his wife Margherita in June 1840 and their two children in the two previous years that he almost abandoned his composing career. Thankfully for opera-lovers he changed his mind.

Where to go next

Anyone who enjoys the music of *Rigoletto* will surely be delighted by the three other operas Verdi composed during the same period: *Stiffelio*, a rarely performed masterpiece about a cuckolded preacher, *Il trovatore* and *La traviata*. The musical style in all these works is much like that of *Rigoletto*: tuneful, passionate and dramatic. A similar forthright style can be found in other Italian operas from the generation of composers just before Verdi: the tragedies of Donizetti, for example – such as *Lucia di Lammermoor* or *Lucrezia Borgia* – or the great romantic works of Bellini like *Norma* and his last opera *I Puritani*.

Left A poster for a production of *Aida* at Teatro La Fenice in Venice, 1881.

Verdi's other operas

Verdi composed twenty-eight operas during his long career, all except two of them tragedies.

NABUCCO

Opera in four acts
Libretto by Temistocle Solera after Anicet-Bourgeois
and Francis Cornue's play, Nabucodonosor
Original language Italian
First performed in Milan, 1842
Approximate length 135 minutes

Verdi's third opera and first great success is particularly well known for the longing chorus of the Hebrew Slaves. The plot concerns the Assyrian leader Nabucco and his fight against the Israelites, focusing on the rivalry between his daughters Fenena and the scheming Abigaille for the love of the Israelite leader Ismaele.

IL TROVATORE (The Troubadour)

Opera in four acts
Libretto by Salvatore Cammarano and Leone
Emanuele Bardare after Antonio Garcia
Gutierrez's El Trovador
Original language Italian
First performed in Rome, 1853
Approximate length 135 minutes

One of Verdi's most tuneful and exciting operas with, sadly, one of his silliest plots. The vengeful Conte di Luna executes the troubadour Manrico, whom he believes to be the son of the nuisance gypsy, Azucena. He is angry that the girl he loves (Leonora) is interested only in Manrico. After his execution the Conte realizes that Manrico was none other than his own brother whom he had wrongly assumed was murdered by Azucena many years earlier.

LA TRAVIATA (The Wayward Woman)

Opera in three acts
Libretto by Francesco Maria Piave after Alexandre
Dumas' play, La Dame aux Camélias
Original language Italian
First performed in Venice, 1853
Approximate length 120 minutes

Perhaps the most popular of all Verdi's operas. The simple tale of a young nobleman (Alfredo) and his love

for a consumptive courtesan (Violetta) is full of pathos and bitter tragedy. In a deeply moving duet, Alfredo's father persuades Violetta to separate from Alfredo for the sake of his son's happiness and reputation. The lovers are briefly reunited before she dies. The famous drinking song in Act I and the recurring theme of Violetta and Alfredo's love duet are very memorable.

DON CARLOS
Opera in five or four acts
Libretto by Joseph Méry and Camille du Locle after Schiller's play, **Don Carlos**
Original languages French and Italian
First performed in Paris, 1867 and Milan, 1884
Approximate length 180 minutes

Don Carlos was commissioned by the opera house in Paris and is often performed in French, as it was originally written, in a grand five-act version. The Italian version, reduced to four acts and known as *Don Carlo*, is equally popular. In this great moody masterpiece Carlos finds himself up against his father, King Philip II of Spain, when first his beloved Elisabeth is taken from him to be married to Philip and then his execution is ordered for aiding the people of Flanders against the tyranny of their Spanish rulers. Carlos's friendship with Rodrigo, the Marquis of Posa, is of central significance.

AIDA
Opera in four acts
Original language Italian
Libretto by Antonio Ghislanzoni after Camille du Locle
First performed in Cairo, 1871
Approximate length 150 minutes

Verdi's intimate yet spectacular grand opera *Aida* was first performed at the new opera house in Cairo. Radamès, the Egyptian General, is walled up in a tomb after he is

Opposite Violetta throws a party in Act I of *La traviata* at La Scala in Milan. **Above** The soprano Mirella Freni as Elisabeth in *Don Carlos* at the Metropolitan Opera House, New York.

overheard unwittingly passing military secrets to his sweetheart Aida, a slave girl employed by the jealous Amneris. Aida sneaks into the tomb, however, so that she can die with the man she loves. Amneris is one of the most demanding and intense mezzo-soprano roles Verdi ever wrote. The Triumphal March from Act II is a popular orchestral concert piece.

OTELLO
Opera in four acts
Libretto by Arrigo Boito after Shakespeare's play, **Othello**
Original language Italian
First performed in Milan, 1887
Approximate length 135 minutes

This brilliantly concise and moving operatic adaptation of Shakespeare's play is regarded by many as Verdi's finest work. The jealous Iago, overlooked for promotion, dishonestly persuades Otello that his wife Desdemona is having an affair with the promoted officer, Cassio. Otello, blindly believing him, strangles Desdemona, discovering the truth about Iago's deceit only when it is too late.

FALSTAFF
Opera in three acts
Libretto by Arrigo Boito after Shakespeare's play,
The Merry Wives of Windsor
Original language Italian
First performed in Milan, 1893
Approximate length 120 minutes

Verdi's "mighty burst of laughter" was only his second comedy but his last opera, finished when the composer was just over eighty years old. The ridiculous, pompous, conceited but ultimately likable Sir John Falstaff is twice humiliated after it is discovered that he has sent the same love letter to two different married women. First he is thrown into the river in a dirty linen basket, then made to look a fool by being forced to wear antlers in Hearn Wood. When brilliantly performed Falstaff is truly one of the funniest of all comic operas.

WAGNER:
DIE MEISTERSINGER VON NÜRNBERG

CD tracks 36 (timeline) and **37**

The Mastersingers of Nuremberg
Opera in *three acts*
Music by *Richard Wagner*
Libretto by *Richard Wagner*
Original language *German*
First performed in *Munich, 1868*
Approximate length *260 minutes*

Wagner's *Die Meistersinger* may not be his shortest opera (that honour goes to *Der fliegende Holländer* – The Flying Dutchman – at just over two hours) but it is probably the most approachable for those who do not know his music. The popularity of *Die Meistersinger* during Wagner's lifetime was due in part to the nationalist fervour it engendered in the approach to the Franco-Prussian war. Today the attraction of the opera lies in its rich and seamless orchestration, an abundant sense of comic satire and many sublimely inspired melodies. In these respects, *Die Meistersinger* is not perhaps typical of Wagner's style, but it serves as a useful introduction to Wagner nonetheless.

Summary of the plot

A young Franconian knight, Walther von Stolzing, is in love with Eva, but to claim her hand he must join the Guild of Mastersingers and win the forthcoming singing competition. With the help of the cobbler and poet, Hans Sachs, he composes and sings

Walther offers his "Preislied" (Prize Song) to the assembled crowd in the great climax of Wagner's opera, *Die Meistersinger*, produced at Sadler's Wells Theatre in London.

a song that does indeed win him the competition by appealing to the hearts of the people rather than the intellects of the other guildsmen. His chief adversary is the petty-minded stickler of a town clerk, Sixtus Beckmesser (a satiric parody of the powerful anti-Wagnerian music critic, Edouard Hanslick), who by the end has been suitably humiliated, snubbed and beaten to give Walther's eventual song-contest victory an added glow.

A brief history of the opera

Wagner first planned the scenario for *Die Meistersinger* in 1845, imagining it as a companion piece to his earlier opera *Tannhäuser*, which also featured a song contest. In the event, the opera he composed during much of the 1860s became broader and more philosophical than he had first conceived. Wagner researched many aspects of life and custom in sixteenth-century Nuremberg. He investigated the practices of the old singing guilds and read about folk traditions and local history to paint as accurate a picture as possible. The story, however, was largely of Wagner's own invention – although the central idea of an artist winning a competition by breaking the rules is an old one. The first performance was conducted by the distinguished Hans von Bülow who was later to lose his wife, Cosima, to Wagner. The opera was an instant and resounding success. Its popularity suffered a setback in the first half of the twentieth century when it was designated the official opera of the Nuremberg party congresses by Hitler, who believed its overtly German tone reflected the spirit of his Nazi idealism, but it has since found favour again and is widely performed.

DRAMATIS PERSONAE

Walther von Stolzing a knight
from Franconia . . . . tenor
David apprentice to Hans Sachs . . . . . . tenor
Eva Pogner's daughter . . . . soprano
Magdalene Eva's companion . . . . soprano
A night watchman . . . . bass

The Mastersingers:
Hans Sachs cobbler . . . . bass-baritone
Veit Pogner goldsmith . . . . bass
Sixtus Beckmesser town clerk . . . . . . bass
Kunz Vogelgesang furrier . . . . tenor
Konrad Nachtiggal tinsmith . . . . bass
Fritz Kothner baker . . . . bass
Balthasar Zorn pewterer . . . . tenor
Ulrich Eisslinger grocer . . . . tenor
Augustin Moser tailor . . . . tenor
Hermann Ortel soapmaker . . . . bass
Hans Schwarz stocking weaver . . . . . . bass
Hans Foltz coppersmith . . . . bass

Choruses of citizens, journeymen, guild members, apprentices and others

Setting Nuremberg in the middle of the sixteenth century

The "Preislied" and other highlights

The overture to *Die Meistersinger*, with its naturally evolving string of robust tunes and bustling atmosphere depicting the busy lives of the people of Nuremberg, is justly famous as an orchestral piece in its own right. The overture and Act I took Wagner six and a half years to

0.01 The "Preislied" (prize song) is the climax of the opera: Walther is hoping to win the song contest and thus the hand in marriage of his beloved Eva. The opening woodwind chord (echoed at 0.09 by the strings) is to allow the tension to mount and give Walther time to draw breath.

0.20 Walther, sung by Ben Heppner, begins his song with a great sense of purpose, doubled by a clarinet.

0.29 Violins take up the tune, giving a warmer feel. The orchestral texture becomes increasingly rich, with more instruments coming in all the time, as Walther grows in confidence. Listen too for the harp, which is often used musically to evoke images of paradise.

"Morgenlich... von Blüt' und Duft geschwellt die Luft, voll aller Wonnen...

Franz Nachbaur as Walther in the world premiere of *Die Meistersinger* in Munich on 21 June 1868.

■ Walther

"Morgenlich leuchtend im rosigen Schein, von Blüt' und Duft geschwellt die Luft, voll aller Wonnen nie ersonnen, ein Garten lud mich ein, dort unter einem Wunderbaum, von Früchten reich behangen, zu schau'n im sel'gen Liebestraum, was höchstem Lustverlangen Erfüllung kühn verhiess, das schönste Weib, Eva im Paradies."

"Shining in the rosy light of morning, the air heavy with blossom and scent, full of every inexpressible joy, a garden beckoned me to enter and beneath a magnificent tree there, with richly hanging fruit, to behold in a blessed dream of love, boldly promising fulfilment to the highest of joy's desires, the most beautiful woman: Eva in Paradise!" ·

■ The People

Das ist was and'res.
Wer hätt's gedacht?
Was doch recht
Wort und Vortrag macht!

That's another matter!
Who'd have guessed?
What a difference the words and delivery make!

■ The Mastersingers

Jawohl! Ich merk'! 's ist ein ander Ding, ob falsch man oder richtig sing'.

Yes, indeed! I see! It makes a difference if one sings it wrong or right.

■ Sachs

Zeuge am Ort! Fahret fort!

Witness, continue!

■ Walther

"Abendlich dämmernd umschloss mich die Nacht;

"In the evening twilight night enfolded me;

I.21 Walther takes on a much more tender tone here as he speaks of Eva, with whom he is in love. Note how the music becomes more gentle too: he is accompanied softly by the orchestra.

I.28 The people and Master-singers interrupt, full of praise for Walther. They attempt to talk softly, but the volume slowly increases in their general excitement.

I.44 Sachs comes in to bid Walther to continue. He is accompanied by the flute.

I.52 Walther is talking of evening shadows, so rather than being doubled as he was in the first verse by clarinets (perhaps representing the dawn chorus), he is here accompanied by the rich sound of violas and cellos.

...zu schau'n im...   Erfüllung kühn...   Eva in Paradies."   "Abendlich...

Zeuge am Ort...

Das ist was and'res...

Jawohl! Ich merk'! 's ist ein...

The town of Nuremburg, where *Die Meistersinger* is set, in a painting of about 1515–20.

complete, which was a long time even by Wagner's standards. The style that Wagner adopted for this work was different from that of *Tristan und Isolde* or any of his previous operas. In *Die Meistersinger*, Wagner succeeded in forging a new style to suit his archaic subject, moving closer to German popular music while continuing to compose music that his contemporaries would have recognized as idiomatically distinct.

Although strands of the "Preislied" (prize song) are first heard in the overture, the melody and its accompaniment grow during the course of the opera, culminating in Walther's breathtaking final rendition (**CD track 36**, and see also the "timeline"). To compose a four-hour opera about a song contest is a risk, and Wagner realized that the winning song would have to be absolutely breathtaking if the opera

2.18 Walther is supposed to be breaking the pedantic traditions of the mastersingers in this song. This is reflected in the music, as one phrase grows organically out of another. The song seems to be a real expression of his innermost desires.

2.22 Walther is doubled by an oboe.

2.51 An echo of the close of the previous verse – although this time he is accompanied by woodwind, and the pitch rises at the end.

...auf steilem Pfad war ich genaht... Dort unter einem Lorbeerbaum, von Sternen hell... die Muse...."

Wagner based Hans Sachs on a real historical figure. Sachs was a member of Nuremberg's sixteenth-century guild of Mastersingers. This engraving of him dates from 1545.

■ Walther

auf steilem Pfad war ich genaht
zu einer Quelle reiner Welle,
die lockend mir gelacht:
Dort unter einem Lorbeerbaum,
von Sternen hell durchscheinen,
ich schaut' im wachen Dichtertraum
von heilig holden Mienen,
mich netzend mit dem edlen Nass,
das hehrste Weib:
die Muse des Parnass."

on a steep path I had approached
a spring of pure water,
which laughed enticingly at me:
there beneath a laurel-tree,
with stars shining brightly through its leaves,
in a poet's waking dream I beheld,
holy and fair of countenance,
and sprinkling me with the precious water,
the most wonderful woman:
the Muse of Parnassus!"

■ The People

So hold und traut, wie fern es schwebt,
doch ist's als ob man's mit erlebt!

So gracious and familiar, however far it soars,
but we seem to be experiencing it with him!

■ The Mastersingers

's ist kühn und seltsam, das ist wahr:
Doch wohlgereimt und singebar.

It's bold and strange, that's true:
but it rhymes well and is singable.

■ Sachs

Zeuge wohl erkiest!
Fahret fort und schliesst!

Well-chosen witness!
Continue and conclude!

■ Walther

"Huldreichster Tag, dem ich aus
Dichters Traum erwacht!
Das ich erträumt, das Paradies,
in himmlisch neu verklärter Pracht
hell vor mir lag, dahin lachend nun
der Quell den Pfad mir wies;

"Most blessed day, to which I awoke from
a poet's dream!
The Paradise of which I had dreamed,
and to which the spring laughingly now
showed me the path, lay bright before me
in heavenly, new transfigured splendour;

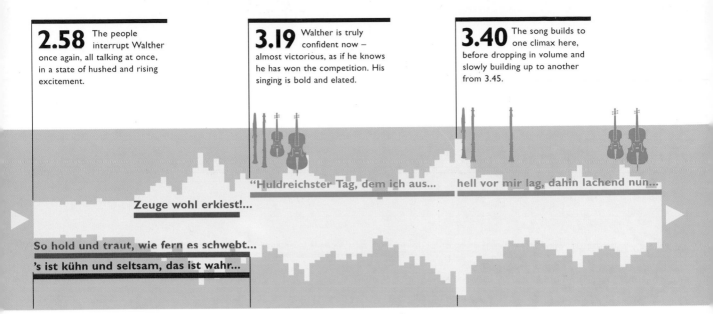

2.58 The people interrupt Walther once again, all talking at once, in a state of hushed and rising excitement.

3.19 Walther is truly confident now – almost victorious, as if he knows he has won the competition. His singing is bold and elated.

3.40 The song builds to one climax here, before dropping in volume and slowly building up to another from 3.45.

"Huldreichster Tag, dem ich aus...

hell vor mir lag, dahin lachend nun...

Zeuge wohl erkiest!...

So hold und traut, wie fern es schwebt...

's ist kühn und seltsam, das ist wahr...

was to avoid being ridiculed. The song he composed was indeed brilliant, the great heroic sweep of its melody and the flowing line of orchestral accompaniment ensuring that the "Preislied" is the emotional climax of every performance. Among the opera's other notable highlights are the crazy riot scene at the end of Act II (CD track 37) and the moving quintet from Act III.

Wagner designed the Festspielhaus at Bayreuth especially for the performance of his own works. He insisted that his last opera *Parsifal* should be performed in no other theatre, but these wishes were ignored soon after his death.

The composer: Richard Wagner (1813–83)

As the unlikely son of a police clerk from Leipzig, Richard Wagner became the most influential composer that ever lived. After a time as a conductor in Germany, he travelled with his wife to Paris where he lived in poverty, hoping (initially in vain) to arouse interest in his works. His first successes were in Dresden with the operas *Rienzi* (1840), *Der fliegende Holländer* (1843) and *Tannhäuser* (1845). After being involved in the Dresden uprising of 1848, he was exiled to Switzerland, where *Der Ring des Nibelungen* was conceived and *Tristan und Isolde*

3.53 Canadian tenor Ben Heppner approaches the climax of his third verse in passionate full voice.

4.21 The people cannot contain their excitement any longer and interrupt Walther before he has finished singing.

4.46 The people echo Walther in a state of hardly containable emotion.

...dort geboren... so heilig ernst als mild, ward kühn von mir gefreit; am...

Gewiegt wie in den schönsten Traum... Riech ihm das Reis!...

Ja, holder Sänger! Nimm das...

The Mexican tenor Francisco Araiza as Walther, singing the Prize Song, in a production of *Die Meistersinger* at the Metropolitan Opera House in New York.

■ Walther

die, dort geboren, mein Herz erkoren,
der Erde lieblischstes Bild,
als Muse mir geweiht,
so heilig ernst als mild,
ward kühn von mir gefreit,
am lichten Tag der Sonnen
durch Sanges Sieg gewonnen
Parnass und Paradies!"

she, born there, my heart's elect,
earth's most lovely picture,
destined to be my Muse,
as holy and grave as she is mild,
was boldly wooed by me,
in the sun's bright daylight,
through victory in song, I had won
Parnassus and Paradise!"

■ The People

Gewiegt wie in den schönsten Traum,
hör ich es wohl, doch fass' es kaum!
[*zu Eva*] Reich ihm das Reis!
Sein der Preis!
Keiner wie er zu werben weiss!

Lulled as if in the most beautiful dream
I hear it well, but scarcely grasp it!
[*to Eva*] Give him the wreath,
The prize is his.
No one can woo like him!

■ The Mastersingers

Ja, holder Sänger! Nimm das Reis!
Dein Sang erwarb dir Meisterpreis!

Yes, gracious singer, take the wreath!
Your song has won you the Master's prize!

■ Pogner

O Sachs! Dir dank' ich Glück und Ehr',
vorüber nun all' Herzbeschwer'!

O Sachs! I owe you happiness
and honour.
Past are now all the cares of my heart!

■ Eva

Keiner wie du so hold zu werben
weiss!

No one can woo as graciously as you!

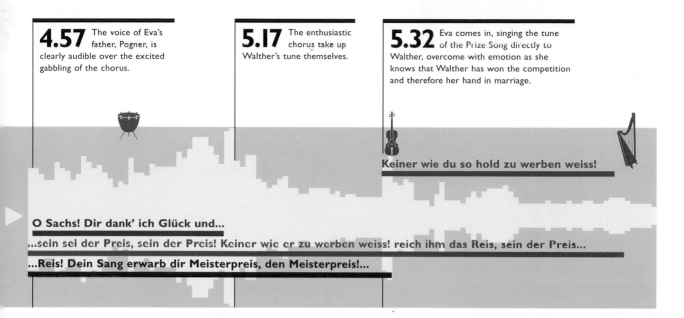

4.57 The voice of Eva's father, Pogner, is clearly audible over the excited gabbling of the chorus.

5.17 The enthusiastic chorus take up Walther's tune themselves.

5.32 Eva comes in, singing the tune of the Prize Song directly to Walther, overcome with emotion as she knows that Walther has won the competition and therefore her hand in marriage.

Keiner wie du so hold zu werben weiss!

O Sachs! Dir dank' ich Glück und...

...sein sei der Preis, sein der Preis! Keiner wie er zu werben weiss! reich ihm das Reis, sein der Preis...

...Reis! Dein Sang erwarb dir Meisterpreis, den Meisterpreis!...

was completed. His private life was never free from scandal and his numerous affairs only resolved themselves after his wife's death in 1866 when Cosima von Bülow (Liszt's daughter, and wife of the conductor Hans von Bülow) set up home with him at Tribschen, on Lake Lucerne in central Switzerland. In 1872 Wagner started work on the building of a new opera house in the Bavarian city of Bayreuth, specially designed to stage his operas. In many of his endeavours he was financially assisted by King Ludwig II of Bavaria, who was a great admirer of his music. Wagner died in the winter of 1883 in Venice.

Wagner as librettist

Wagner's forceful ego would never have allowed him to collaborate with anyone else on a libretto, but his philosophy of a synthesized art form (the *Gesamtkunstwerk*), his natural enjoyment of words and his ability to write well enabled him to produce the librettos to all his musical dramas: in fact, he was one of the earliest composers to provide his own librettos. His language, like his music, is rich and poetic, laden with symbols and layers of meaning. Wagner's greatest achievement as a librettist was his single-minded rejection of established forms and his development of long, complex, unrhymed verses that ideally suited his unique style of "endless melody."

Richard Wagner in 1871, three years after the premiere of *Die Meistersinger*.

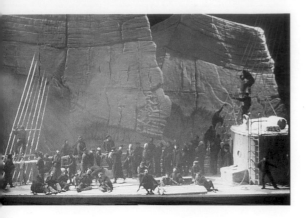

Where to go next

Das Rheingold (Part One of the Ring) and *Der fliegende Holländer* are Wagner's two shortest operas, making them good introductions to his work. Richard Strauss's *Der Rosenkavalier* is a natural successor to *Die Meistersinger* and, despite its length, has justly established itself as the most successful twentieth-century German opera.

Left A scene from Act I of *Der fliegende Holländer* at the Metropolitan Opera House in New York, with a large iceberg as a backdrop.

Other operas by Wagner

Wagner's operas are all strong works: although not immediately accessible, dedicated listening pays great dividends.

DER FLIEGENDE HOLLANDER
(The Flying Dutchman)
Opera in three acts
*Libretto by **Wagner** after **Heine's** version of the legend*
*Original language **German***
*First performed in **Dresden, 1843***
*Approximate length **135 minutes***

In the earliest of Wagner's operas to have gained a permanent foothold in the repertoire, a Dutch sea captain is condemned by the Devil to sail around the world until Judgment Day, being allowed to stop only once every seven years. To break the curse upon him, he must succeed in winning the love of a faithful woman. At a Norwegian port in 1650 the Dutchman sees hope in the young and beautiful Senta, but when he overhears her rejecting her suitor, he believes her faithless and sets sail. She, however, leaps off the cliffs in pursuit of him. The curse is lifted and the two figures are seen mysteriously ascending together into heaven.

TANNHAUSER
Opera in three acts
*Libretto by **Wagner** after a thirteenth-century poem*
*Original language **German***
*First performed in **Dresden, 1845***
*Approximate length **195 minutes***

In Wagner's tale of conflict between sensuality and asceticism, Tannhäuser returns from the sensual world of Venusberg to be reunited with his pining sweetheart, Elisabeth. During a song contest in praise of love, Tannhäuser disgraces himself by shouting in praise of the pleasures of Venus. After the Pope refuses to absolve him, Tannhäuser contemplates a return to Venusberg. Elisabeth dies of a broken heart and Tannhäuser falls dead beside her, saved at the final hour by a mystic chorus of pilgrims.

LOHENGRIN
Opera in three acts
*Libretto by **Wagner** after an anonymous German epic*
*Original language **German***
*First performed in **Weimar, 1850***
*Approximate length **220 minutes***

The mysterious knight, Lohengrin, arrives on a swan-drawn boat, bringing hope to the strife-riven kingdom of Brabant. He promises to marry Elsa as long as she does not ask him his name. After slaying a Brabant count in self defence, however, Lohengrin feels obliged to reveal his true identity as a knight of the Holy Grail. He departs the kingdom and the sorrowful Elsa, this time in a boat drawn by a dove. Wagner's music for this fanciful story indicates an early move towards the seamless style of his later years.

TRISTAN UND ISOLDE
Opera in three acts
*Original language **German***
*Libretto by **Wagner** after legend*
*First performed in **Munich, 1865***
*Approximate length **225 minutes***

Partly influenced by Wagner's frustrated love for the wife of his patron, this is his most passionate work. Tristan, bringing Isolde by sea from Ireland to be married to his master, King Marke of Cornwall, falls uncontrollably in love after inadvertently swallowing a love potion. When the two are caught embracing, Tristan is banished. After he has been mortally wounded by the scheming knight, Melot, the secret of the potion is revealed. Tristan is forgiven before he dies and Isolde, in her famous "Liebestod," prays to be united with Tristan in death.

DER RING DES NIBELUNGEN
(The Ring of the Nibelung)

Operatic tetralogy
*Libretto by **Wagner** after legend*
*Original language **German***
*First performed in **Munich, 1869** (Das Rheingold),*
Munich, 1870 (Die Walküre), Bayreuth, 1876
(Siegfried and Götterdämmerung)
Approximate length 14–15 hours

Wagner's epic drama, set in four parts, is quite unique in the history of opera. Rich in musical and literary symbolism, the work can be enjoyed on many levels; at its simplest it is a fairy tale. Part One (*Das Rheingold*, The Rhinegold) tells the story of the evil dwarf, Alberich, who steals gold guarded by the Rhinemaidens (for whoever forges a ring from the gold will enjoy total power). But the gold is tricked from him by Wotan, King of the Gods, who pays it reluctantly to two giants in return for building his palace, Valhalla. In Part Two of the Ring (*Die Walküre*, The Valkyrie) the hero Siegfried is conceived by brother and sister, Siegmund and Sieglinde. Wotan imprisons his favourite daughter Brünnhilde in a ring of fire for defying his order that Siegmund be killed. She can only be released by a hero brave enough to break through the flames. Part Three (*Siegfried*) follows the young hero as he obtains the gold by slaying the giant Fafner and releases Brünnhilde from her captivity, while in the final part (*Götterdämmerung*, Twilight of the Gods), Siegfried reluctantly leaves Brünnhilde in search of adventure and is tricked with the aid of a magic potion

into falling in love with Gutrune. Brünnhilde is devastated. After Siegfried is murdered with her connivance, she rides her horse into his funeral pyre. Valhalla is destroyed by flame and flood as the Rhinemaidens reclaim their precious ring.

PARSIFAL

Opera in three acts
*Original language **German***
*Libretto by **Wagner** mainly after Eschenbach*
*First performed in **Bayreuth, 1882***
Approximate length 260 minutes

Wagner's last opera is a quasi-religious experience. While the slow, cathartic music is unquestionably beautiful and effective, the exact meaning of the story has remained a subject of heated debate ever since its Bayreuth premiere in 1882. It is predicted that a young hero, "a blameless fool made wise through compassion," will one day come to save the wounded knight, Amfortas, and himself become King of the Grail. Parsifal fits the bill by confounding the evil magician Klingsor and rejecting the sexual advances of the wild woman, Kundry. He is eventually crowned King and heals Amfortas as Kundry dies and a white dove flies up from her body.

Left James Morris as Wotan the Wanderer in a scene from Part Two of the Ring: *Die Walküre.* **Below** The final scene from a production of *Parsifal* at the Royal Opera House in London.

MUSSORGSKY:
BORIS GODUNOV

CD tracks 38 (timeline) and 39

Opera in *four acts*
Music by *Modest Mussorgsky*
Libretto by *Mussorgsky* after *Aleksandr Pushkin*
Original language *Russian*
First performed in *St Petersburg, 1874*
Approximate length *195 minutes*

Boris Godunov, Mussorgsky's only completed opera, is astonishing for the power of its emotion, the clarity and startling originality of its music and the great binding choruses that give the work such cohesion, epic weight and burning appeal. In *Boris Godunov* the chorus, which represents the oppressed Russian people, is elevated almost to the status of a principal character. The technique of dividing the chorus into individual groups expressing their own thoughts is a masterful innovation from a composer who had next to no compositional experience and was working in a restrictive and censorious political climate. Above all, it is Mussorgsky's intensely psychological portrait of the guilt-ridden Boris – a real historical character – that truly sets this work apart from that of other Russian composers of the time.

Summary of the plot

Rumours abound that Boris (regent to the feeble Russian Tsar, Fyodor) was responsible for the murder of the Tsar's half-brother and legitimate heir, the Tsarevitch Dmitri, who was found dying from a knife wound. After Fyodor's death Boris is crowned Tsar, but as time passes he becomes racked with guilt and tension about the Tsarevitch. Things are brought to a head by the young monk, Grigory, who – obsessed with a desire for greatness and realizing that he is the same age as the missing Tsarevitch – pretends to be Dmitri and sets out to challenge Boris. Boris's worries have by now got the better of him and he is not even sure himself whether Dmitri is alive or dead. Boris dies of a seizure after a moving monologue to his son. In the final scene,

Tsar Boris Godunov, who ruled Russia from 1598 to 1605, and on whom Mussorgsky's opera is based.

the false Dmitri leads a large crowd of credulous supporters into Moscow as a holy simpleton laments the onset of troubled times for Russia.

A brief history of the opera

Mussorgsky's enthusiasm for Pushkin's historical drama *Boris Godunov* (published in 1831) encouraged him to break off from his experimental setting of Nikolai Gogol's *The Marriage* and explore the operatic possibilities of *Boris Godunov* instead. Mussorgsky was not the only composer to find inspiration in Aleksandr Pushkin (1799–1837). All of the greatest Russian composers have based operas on his stories, among the most famous being Mikhail Glinka's *Ruslan and Lyudmila*, Nikolai Rimsky-Korsakov's *Tsar Saltan* and *The Golden Cockerel*, Pyotr Ilyich Tchaikovsky's *Queen of Spades* and *Eugene Onegin*, Sergei Rachmaninov's *Aleko* and *The Miserly Knight* and Igor Stravinsky's *Mavra*.

Mussorgsky managed to reduce Pushkin's twenty-five-scene structure to a mere seven scenes and immediately began his composition, finishing with breathtaking speed in less than a year in October 1868. Due to a number of adverse factors, particularly the fear of censorship, novelty and the lack of a principal female role, the opera was at first rejected by the Maryinsky Theatre in St Petersburg. Major revisions followed, however, including the addition of a whole new act (Act III or the Polish Act) that provided the leading female part of Princess Marina. The final version is now regarded as the definitive version, and from its first performance in 1874 it has continued to prove a powerful and popular work both in Russia and internationally. The success of the work today is largely due to Mussorgksy's extraordinary flair for creating atmosphere and drawing character with music.

DRAMATIS PERSONAE

Boris Godunov . . . . bass
Xenia his daughter . . . . soprano
Fyodor his son . . . . mezzo-soprano
Grigory (the Pretender) . . . . tenor
Pimen a monk and chronicler . . . . bass
Prince Vassily Ivanovich Shuisky . . . tenor
Andrei Shchelkalov . . . . baritone
Princess Marina . . . . soprano/mezzo

14 other soloists (minor roles)

Chorus of boyars, their children, musketeers, royal bodyguards, police officers, blind pilgrims, Muscovites

Setting Russia and Poland, 1598–1605

The coronation scene from Act I of *Boris Godunov* (see "timeline" overleaf).

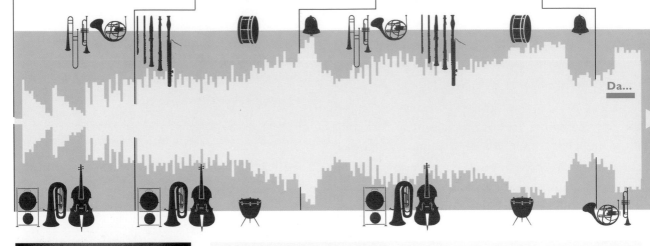

0.01 The gong announces the arrival of the royal procession. A slow, processional beat is created by the brass and percussion. Brass instruments are often used on state occasions.

0.27 Rumours abound that Boris has murdered the Tsarevitch, so although the tone is celebratory, there is an undercurrent of fear and mistrust. The low bass notes sound sinister.

1.03 Church bells ring outside the cathedral. The music becomes faster and more chaotic all the time, suggesting excitement, bustle and a slight feeling of panic.

2.04 A brass fanfare heralds Prince Shuisky who carries the Tsar's crown on a cushion.

Da...

The composer, Modest Mussorgsky. Although his only completed opera, *Boris Godunov*, was at first dismissed by the critics, it was immediately popular with the audience.

■ **Prince Shuisky**
Da zdrávstvuet tsar Boris Feódorovich!   Long live Tsar Boris Fyodorovich!

■ **The People**
Zhiví i zdrávstvuy,   Long live and prosper
tsar nash bátyushka!   Our father, the Tsar!

■ **Prince Shuisky**
Slávte!   Praise him!

■ **The People**
Uzh kak na nyébye sóntsu krásnomu   As we praise the magnificent sun in
Sláva, Sláva!   the sky, Glory, Glory!
Uzh i kak na Rusí tsaryú Borísu   So we praise Tsar Boris of Russia,
Zhiví i zdrávstvuy!   Long live and prosper,
Tsar nash bátyushka!   Our father, the Tsar!
Ráduysya lyud!   Rejoice everyone,
Ráduysya, veselísya lyud!   Everyone rejoice and make merry.
Pravoslávny lyud!   True believers!
Velicháy tsaryá Borísa i slav!   Exalt and glorify Tsar Boris!

■ **The Boyars**
Da zdrávstvuet!   Long live Tsar Boris Fyodorovich!

■ **The People**
Da zdrávstvuet!   Long may he live!
Uzh kak na Rusí tsaryú Borísu   Glory to Boris, the Tsar of all Russia!
Sláva!   Glory!

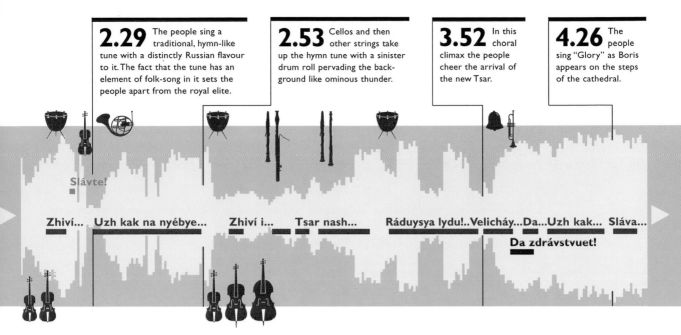

2.29 The people sing a traditional, hymn-like tune with a distinctly Russian flavour to it. The fact that the tune has an element of folk-song in it sets the people apart from the royal elite.

2.53 Cellos and then other strings take up the hymn tune with a sinister drum roll pervading the background like ominous thunder.

3.52 In this choral climax the people cheer the arrival of the new Tsar.

4.26 The people sing "Glory" as Boris appears on the steps of the cathedral.

Slávte!

Zhiví... Uzh kak na nyébye... Zhiví i... Tsar nash... Ráduysya lyudu!.. Velicháy...Da...Uzh kak... Sláva...

Da zdrávstvuet!

The coronation scene and other highlights

In the second scene and great choral section of the opera (featured on **CD track 38** and decoded on the "timeline" above), the crowd in Kremlin Square generate a false sense of jubilation about Boris's coronation. The new Tsar expresses humility and hints at his fear of some imminent doom. For the "Coronation chorus" Mussorgsky borrowed from an old Russian fortune-telling song, apparently only because it happened to use the word "Glory!" in its refrain. Other highlights include the "Chorus of Polish Maidens" and Marina's aria and duet from the belatedly incorporated third act; Boris's great conscience-examining soliloquy from Act II; his crushingly sad farewell to his son before he dies; and the very end, in which a simpleton laments Russia's misfortunes (**CD track 39**).

The composer: Modest Mussorgsky (1839–81)

Mussorgsky had a difficult time gaining the acceptance and recognition of his peers. His mood swings (from boastful self-confidence to complete despair) and the alcoholic fits

A view of Moscow painted in 1839, the year of Mussorgsky's birth.

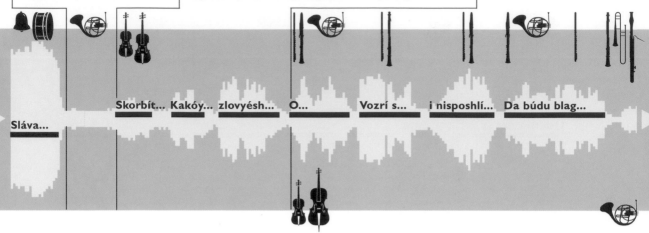

4.35 A single horn links the chorus to Boris's first entry, allowing the ears of the audience to adjust from the massive clamour of the people's voices to the thoughts and fears of one man.

4.47 The voice of Martti Talvela, playing Boris on this recording, is very rich and soulful, as if the words were coming from the depths of his heart. It is quite rare for a title role to be a bass, but Mussorgsky probably chose this kind of voice as it is more weighty and perhaps more expressive of fear than a tenor. The music drags down, giving a feeling of depression and impending doom.

5.24 The aria takes on a prayer-like tone. The melodic accompaniment is high, perhaps suggesting heaven.

Sláva... Skorbít... Kakóy... zlovyésh... O... Vozrí s... i nisposhlí... Da búdu blag...

This stage design for the coronation scene from *Boris Godunov* was produced by M. I. Bocharov for the first performance of the opera in St Petersburg in 1874.

that eventually killed him conspired to present Mussorgsky to many people as something of an inspired amateur. But it was his musical style as much as his attitude that earned him so much disapproval. The composer César Cui commented in 1874: "These are the chief defects of *Boris Godunov*: chopped recitative and looseness of musical discourse, resulting in the effect of a potpourri.... These defects are the consequence of immaturity, and an undiscriminating, self-complacent, hasty method of composition." Tchaikovsky was also unimpressed by the opera and wrote in a letter to his brother: "I consign *Boris* from the bottom of my heart to the devil; it is the most insipid and base parody on music." Even Mussorgsky's teacher described him as "almost a total idiot." Despite his defects, Mussorgsky is recognized today as a composer of uniquely inspired music.

Much of his professional career was taken up not with music but first with the cadet guards and then the Russian civil service. Of his six operas only *Boris Godunov* was actually finished by the composer: all the rest were left in various states of incompletion and disarray when he died.

6.49 Boris turns to face the crowd and changes his tone to one of good cheer as he invites the people to a banquet.

7.15 The people start singing again, giving a sense of musical balance to the whole scene.

7.34 The accompaniment is quite unsettled, even a little frightening. The full orchestra, with heavy brass and bells, adds to the weight.

8.40 A great drum roll ends the scene on an ominous note, as if dark clouds were coming over.

Tepér...a tam...vsyekh...vsyem...

Sláva... Zhiví... Mnólgaya... Uzh... Uzh kak... Sláva... Sláva...

■ Boris

Skorbít dusha!
Kakóy-to strakh nevól'ny
zlovyéshchim predchúvstviem
skovál mnye syérdtse.
O, právednik,
o moy otyéts derzhávny!
Vozri s nebyés
na slyózy vyérnykh slug
i nisposhlí to mnye svyshchénnoye
na vlast blagoslovyénye:
Da búdu blag i práveden kak ty,
da v slávye právlyu svoy naród.
Tepér poklónimsa
pochíyushchim vlastítelyam Rusíi,
a tam szyvát' naród na pir,
vsyekh, ot boyár do níshchevo sleptsá:
vsyem vól'ny vkhod,
vsye gósti dorogíye.

My soul is sad,
An irresistible fear
has seized my heart
with a sense of evil foreboding.
O Righteous God,
Father almighty!
Look down from heaven
on the tears of Thy faithful servant
and send me a holy blessing
for my reign.
Let me be good and righteous, as You are;
May I rule over my people in glory.
Now let us pay our respects to the
past rulers of Russia now deceased.
And now we invite the people to a feast,
All, from boyar to blind beggar,
Everyone is welcome.
Come dear guests.

■ The People

Sláva, Sláva, Sláva!
Zhiví i zdrástvuy,
tsar nash bátyushka!
Mnólgaya lyéta tsaryú Borísu!
Uzh kak na nyébye sólnyshku
Sláva! Sláva!
Uzh kak na Rusí tsaryú Borísu
Sláva! Sláva i mnógaya lyéta!

Glory, Glory, Glory!
Long live and prosper
Our father, the Tsar!
Long life to Tsar Boris!
As we praise the sun and sky,
Glory! Glory!
So we praise Tsar Boris of Russia,
Glory! Glory! And long life!

Fyodor Chaliapin as Tsar Boris Godunov. Chaliapin (1873–1938) was one of the greatest Russian basses, and a famous interpreter of the role of Boris.

Above A scene from a 1992 production of Mussorgsky's opera-ballet *Mlada* at the Bolshoi Theatre in Moscow.

Where to go next

Aleksandr Borodin's *Prince Igor* is a seminal work of Russian "grand opera" and shares with *Boris Godunov* the sense of epic scale that so often characterizes Russian opera of the nineteenth century. *Khovanshchina*, Mussorgsky's unfinished masterpiece, is perhaps closer in its dark and foreboding atmosphere to *Boris Godunov*. The most popular works of Russian opera are Tchaikovsky's *Eugene Onegin* and *The Queen of Spades*, both of which deal, like *Boris*, with the intense psychology of individuals set in a grand and sweeping framework of Russian society. Other important works of Russian "grand opera" include Glinka's *Ruslan and Lyudmila*, Prokofiev's *The Fiery Angel* and *War and Peace* and *Lady Macbeth of Mtsensk* by Shostakovich.

Other operas by Mussorgsky

With the exception of *Boris Godunov* and *Khovanshchina*, Mussorgsky's operas are very rarely performed outside Russia. Recordings of most of them are available, however.

SALAMMBO

Opera in four acts
*Libretto by **Mussorgsky** after **Gustave Flaubert***
*Original language **Russian***
*Composed between **1863** and **1866***
*First performed in **Milan, 1989***
*Approximate length **90 minutes***

Six scenes survive from Mussorgsky's earliest attempt at full-length opera, three of them scored for orchestra. The exotic oriental story is taken from Flaubert's novel *Salammbô* about ancient Carthage, and Mussorgsky later adapted parts of the musical score for *Boris Godunov*.

THE MARRIAGE

Opera in one act
*Libretto by **Mussorgsky** after **Nikolai Gogol***
*Original language **Russian***
*First performed in **St Petersburg, 1908***
*Approximate length **40 minutes***

The Marriage, like most of Mussorgsky's important works, was left unfinished by the composer. The work was first performed in a version for piano by Rimsky-Korsakov in 1908. Subsequently, it was orchestrated by Aleksandr Galik in 1917 and completed by Mikhail Ippolitov Ivanov in 1931. The story concerns the fussing preparations for a marriage, and Mussorgsky's music, which is non-lyrical, follows the pattern of spoken dialogue. *The Marriage* is the first Russian opera to be composed using a thorough system of thematic leitmotifs.

MLADA

Opera-ballet
*Libretto by **Viktor Krylov***
*Composed in **1872** by **César Cui, Nikolai Rimsky-Korsakov** and **Aleksandr Borodin***

Two pieces by Mussorgsky survive from this strange collaborative effort that was eventually abandoned by everyone involved in it: the "March of the Princes and Priests" and the market scene, later reused as the opening chorus in *Sorochinsky Fair*.

KHOVANSHCHINA (The Khovansky Affair)

Opera in five acts
*Libretto by **Mussorgsky** and **Vladimir Vaily'evich Stasov***
*Original language **Russian***
*First performed in **St Petersburg, 1886***
*Approximate length **180 minutes***

Best known in the versions completed by Rimsky-Korsakov and Dmitri Shostakovich, Mussorgsky's huge epic, *Khovanshchina*, is still regarded as a classic pillar of Russian "grand opera" despite the incomplete state in which Mussorgsky left it. A plot by the seventeenth-century Moscow militia to overthrow the Russian Tsar is doomed

from the beginning when the Tsar is warned of the conspiracy by a public letter writer. At the end of the opera, Old Believers throw themselves on to a funeral pyre much to the horror of Tsarist troops sent to arrest them. Although *Khovanshchina* is closer in style to *Boris Godunov* than any of Mussorgsky's other operas, it still has a driven atmosphere all of its own. The opera was later orchestrated by Ravel and Stravinsky for Diaghilev's ballet company.

Above Costume designs for a production of *Khovanshchina* at the Paris Opéra. **Below** A scene from *Khovanshchina* staged by English National Opera in London.

SOROCHINSKY FAIR

Opera in three acts
Libretto by Mussorgsky after a novel
by Nikolai Gogol
Original language Russian
First performed in St Petersburg, 1911
Approximate length 105 minutes

Left in sketch form only by Mussorgsky when he died, this delightful comedy is now best known in the version completed by the Russian composer Nikolai Tcherepnin. There are other versions, though, notably one by César Cui. The ridiculous plot concerns itself with the Ukrainian family of the beautiful Parasya, whose father wishes her to marry the young peasant Gritsko and whose mother, mainly for snobbish reasons, does not. Her mother is eventually humiliated and the wedding goes ahead. Mussorgsky borrowed music from earlier pieces such as "Night on a Bare Mountain." The jubilant "Gopak" (Ukrainian dance) is a memorable highlight of the opera.

BIZET:
CARMEN

CD tracks 40 (timeline) and 41

Opera in *four acts*
Music by *Georges Bizet*
Libretto by *Henri Meilhac* and *Ludovic Halévy*
after *Prosper Mérimée's* novel, *Carmen*
Original language *French*
First performed in *Paris, 1875*
Approximate length *165 minutes*

Don José (Placido Domingo) and Carmen (Julia Migenes-Johnson) in the last scene of *Carmen* from the 1984 film of the opera.

The audience attending *Carmen*'s premiere at the Paris Opéra-Comique in 1875 must have been shocked by what they saw. Nothing could have prepared them for the violent and "unlady-like" character of the principal role. Never before had such a wayward gypsy woman like this been made the focus of an opera, and neither Bizet nor his librettists did anything to make the drama more palatable. The first half hour, a lively street scene, lulls the audience into thinking they have come for an evening of light bourgeois comedy, but *Carmen* turns out to be something quite different. Today's audiences may not find *Carmen* as shocking as it was to the Parisians of Bizet's day, but the opera survives because of its multitude of memorable tunes, its Spanish flavour and quasi-erotic atmosphere and the compelling characterizations of both Carmen and her desperate lover, Don José.

Summary of the plot
Two girls who work in a cigarette factory in Seville start fighting and are brought into the central square where one of them, the gypsy Carmen, is set under the guard of Corporal Don

104

José. Although he claims to be in love with his childhood sweetheart Micaëla, Don José is immediately captivated by Carmen's dark attractive looks and free spirit. He unties her hands, deliberately allowing her to make an escape. While Carmen is dancing at Lillas Pastia's tavern in Act II, the renowned bullfighter Escamillo enters singing his "Toreador" song. His advances to Carmen are rebuffed: she is waiting for Don José. When Don José arrives she tries to persuade him to desert the army and join her in a smuggling racket. He refuses, but when his senior officer, Zuñiga, arrives hoping to seduce Carmen, a fight between the two men looks imminent. Don José is charged with threatening his superior officer and sees no alternative but to join the smugglers. Carmen, though, soon tires of Don José and looks on Escamillo as a more exciting alternative. In the final scene the rejected, ruined and by now hysterical José seeks his revenge at Escamillo's crowded bullfight. Carmen confronts him outside the bull-ring and, as the crowd cheers Escamillo in the background, José stabs her fatally before giving himself up.

A brief history of the opera

Neither the chorus nor the orchestra at the Opéra-Comique were prepared for Bizet's *Carmen* and after a few rehearsals both threatened a strike on the grounds that it was unsingable and unplayable. The strike was averted – but despite the great enthusiasm for the work from the principal soloists the critics were disparaging, complaining that the opera was "immoral," "overlong" and "scientific." Before the premiere Bizet had hoped for a critical success. "The critics," he said, "make out that I am obscure, complicated, tedious, more fettered by technical skill than lit by inspiration. Well this time I have written a work that is all clarity and vivacity, full of colour and melody." The original production ran for forty-five performances and was widely regarded as a *succès de scandale* by critics and public alike. Only three months later the thirty-six-year-old composer was dead, following two heart attacks, just before the real impact and popularity of *Carmen* had begun to take a hold. Today the work is justly regarded as one of the most appealing operas ever written and is performed with systematic regularity in opera houses all over the world.

DRAMATIS PERSONAE

Carmen a gypsy . . . . mezzo-soprano
Don José a corporal . . . . tenor
Escamillo a bullfighter . . . . . .bass/baritone
Micaëla a country girl . . . . . . soprano
Zuñiga a lieutenant . . . . bass
Moralès a corporal . . . . baritone
Frasquita a gypsy . . . . soprano
Mercédès a gypsy . . . . soprano
Lillas Pastia an innkeeper . . . spoken
Andrès an officer . . . . .tenor

Choruses of soldiers, suitors, cigarette girls, Escamillo's supporters, gypsies, merchants and orange-sellers, police, bullfighters, smugglers and urchins

Setting Seville, around 1820

Costume designs for Escamillo, the bull-fighter, for a production of *Carmen* at the Paris Opera House in 1959.

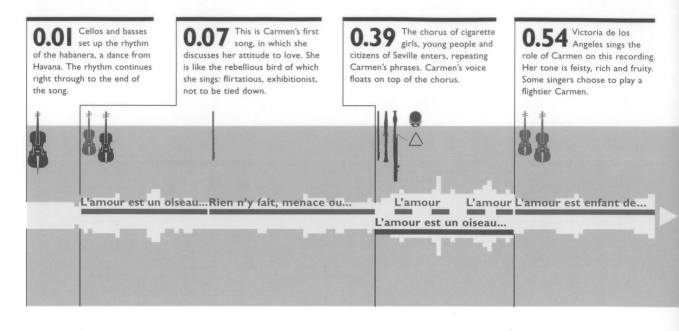

0.01 Cellos and basses set up the rhythm of the habanera, a dance from Havana. The rhythm continues right through to the end of the song.

0.07 This is Carmen's first song, in which she discusses her attitude to love. She is like the rebellious bird of which she sings: flirtatious, exhibitionist, not to be tied down.

0.39 The chorus of cigarette girls, young people and citizens of Seville enters, repeating Carmen's phrases. Carmen's voice floats on top of the chorus.

0.54 Victoria de los Angeles sings the role of Carmen on this recording. Her tone is feisty, rich and fruity. Some singers choose to play a flightier Carmen.

L'amour est un oiseau...Rien n'y fait, menace ou...
L'amour   L'amour   L'amour est enfant de...
L'amour est un oiseau...

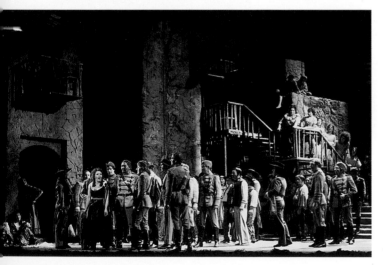

Carmen sings the "Habanera" in a production of the opera by English National Opera in London.

The "Habanera" and other highlights

A habanera is a slow dance of Cuban origin, which found particular favour in Spain. It is the forerunner of many modern dances including the tango. In *Carmen* the famous "Habanera" (**CD track 40**, and see "timeline" above) introduces the title character: it is her first song, and together the words and music perfectly sum up her sensual, gypsy, free-spirited character. The words, reputedly written by Bizet himself, describe love as a free bird, born to a gypsy life, who will fly away as soon she feels trapped. The tripping rhythm of the cellos and basses continues throughout the song, producing a hypnotic effect. Other great highlights from the opera include the manly "Toreador" song that Escamillo sings at the tavern in Act II; Carmen's wild table-top dance for Don José; her seguidilla "Près des remparts de Séville;" Jose's plaintive love-song "La fleur que tu m'avais jetée;" and the death scene at the end (**CD track 41**).

The libretto and its origins

Bizet was commissioned in 1872 to write an opera for the Opéra-Comique in Paris, and as a subject for

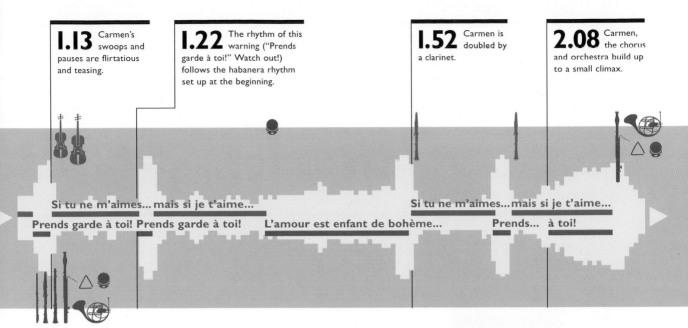

1.13 Carmen's swoops and pauses are flirtatious and teasing.

1.22 The rhythm of this warning ("Prends garde à toi!" Watch out!) follows the habanera rhythm set up at the beginning.

1.52 Carmen is doubled by a clarinet.

2.08 Carmen, the chorus and orchestra build up to a small climax.

Si tu ne m'aimes... mais si je t'aime...

Prends garde à toi! Prends garde à toi!

L'amour est enfant de bohème...

Si tu ne m'aimes... mais si je t'aime...

Prends... à toi!

■ **Carmen**

L'amour est un oiseau rebelle	Love is a rebellious bird
que nul ne peut apprivoiser,	that no one can tame,
et c'est bien en vain qu'on l'appelle,	and it's quite useless to call him
s'il lui convient de refuser.	if it suits him to refuse.
Rien n'y fait, menace ou prière,	Nothing moves him, threat nor plea,
l'un parle bien, l'autre se tait;	one man speaks out, the other is silent
et c'est l'autre que je préfère:	and he's the one I prefer:
il n'a rien dit, mais il me plaît.	he's said nothing, but I like him.

■ **Chorus**

L'amour est un oiseau rebelle...	Love is a rebellious bird...

■ **Carmen**

L'amour est enfant de bohème,	Love is a gypsy child
il n'a jamais connu de loi:	who has never heard of law.
Si tu ne m'aimes pas, je t'aime;	If you do not love me, I love you;
si je t'aime, prends garde à toi!	if I love you, watch out!

■ **Chorus**

Prends garde à toi!	Watch out!
L'amour est enfant de bohème...	Love is a gypsy child...

The mezzo-soprano Muriel Smith in the role of Carmen.

this work he chose a novel by Prosper Mérimée. Several of Mérimée's novels and short stories have been turned into operas but Bizet's *Carmen* is by far the most famous. The French playwright Henri Meilhac and the librettist Ludovic Halévy were responsible for adapting the novel. The partnership between Meilhac and Halévy was one of the most

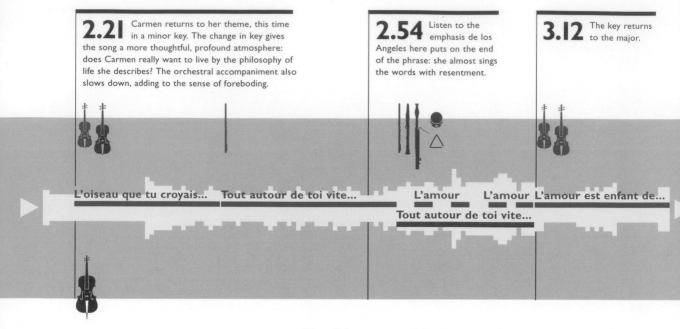

2.21 Carmen returns to her theme, this time in a minor key. The change in key gives the song a more thoughtful, profound atmosphere: does Carmen really want to live by the philosophy of life she describes? The orchestral accompaniment also slows down, adding to the sense of foreboding.

2.54 Listen to the emphasis de los Angeles here puts on the end of the phrase: she almost sings the words with resentment.

3.12 The key returns to the major.

L'oiseau que tu croyais...   Tout autour de toi vite...

L'amour   L'amour L'amour est enfant de...

Tout autour de toi vite...

A set design for the final act of *Carmen*, for the premiere of the opera at the Paris Opera House in 1875.

successful collaborations of the time. Meilhac was considered the witty and fanciful partner while Halévy was admired for his literary skill. They were associated primarily with comic opera and provided Jacques Offenbach with librettos for over twenty years, the most celebrated of these being *La Belle Hélène* (1864) and *La Périchole* (1868). Although the libretto for *Carmen* was in many ways greatly changed from the story Mérimée published in 1845, it retained the essential shockingness of the original work, which was a crucial element in the initial success of the opera.

The composer: Georges Bizet (1838–75)

Bizet composed his first two operas while he was still a student at the Paris Conservatoire. His abilities were soon recognized when he won the prestigious Prix de Rome in the mid 1850s, which enabled him to study in Italy for three years. The Franco-Prussian war, however, together with his marriage to a neurotic wife with an insane mother (respectively the daughter and wife of the distinguished French composer Fromental Halévy), distracted him from his composition and on his death at the youthful age of thirty-six he left a surprisingly small number of finished, mature

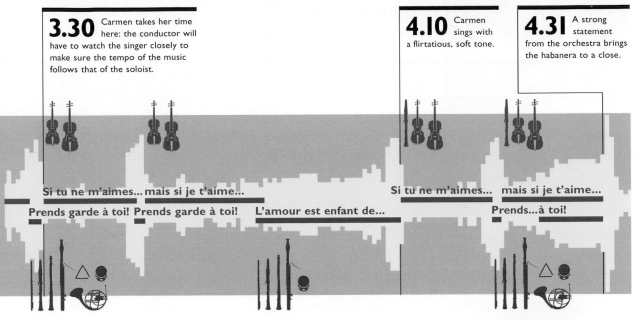

3.30 Carmen takes her time here: the conductor will have to watch the singer closely to make sure the tempo of the music follows that of the soloist.

4.10 Carmen sings with a flirtatious, soft tone.

4.31 A strong statement from the orchestra brings the habanera to a close.

Si tu ne m'aimes... mais si je t'aime...

Prends garde à toi! Prends garde à toi! L'amour est enfant de...

Si tu ne m'aimes... mais si je t'aime...

Prends...à toi!

■ **Carmen**

L'oiseau que tu croyais surprendre	The bird you thought to catch unawares
battit de l'aile et s'envola –	beat its wings and flew away –
l'amour est loin, tu peux l'attendre;	love's far away and you can wait for it;
tu ne l'attends plus, il est là!	you wait for it no longer – and there it is.
Tout autour de toi vite, vite,	All around you, quickly, quickly,
il vient, s'en va, puis il revient –	It comes, It goes, then it returns –
tu crois le tenir, il t'évite,	you think you can hold it, it evades you,
tu crois l'éviter, il te tient.	you think to evade it, it holds you fast.

■ **Chorus**

Tout autour de toi...	All around you...

■ **Carmen**

L'amour est enfant de bohème,	Love is a gypsy child,
il n'a jamais connu de loi.	who has never heard of law.
Si tu ne m'aimes pas, je t'aime;	If you don't love me, I love you;
si je t'aime, prends garde à toi!	if I love you, watch out!
si tu ne m'aimes pas, je t'aime.	If you don't love me, I love you.

■ **Chorus**

Prends garde à toi...	Watch out!
L'amour est enfant de bohème...	Love is a gypsy child...

Georges Bizet, who sadly never lived to enjoy the enormous international success of *Carmen*.

works. During his lifetime he was very much admired by those who knew his work, but like many great composers he suffered from critical neglect and misunderstanding. Today, two of his operas, *Carmen* and *Les pêcheurs de perles*, find themselves in the regular repertory with *Djamileh* and *La jolie fille de Perth* reaching occasional but enthusiastic audiences.

Where to go next

Carmen is an unusual opera in that it wavers between the tragic passions of "grand opera" (as exemplified by the works of Charles Gounod and Giacomo Meyerbeer) and the form and style of the French *opéra comique* (best known today through the works of Jacques Offenbach, a composer who much admired Bizet's work, Louis Ganne and Henri Lecocq). Offenbach's *Les contes d'Hoffmann* shares something of *Carmen*'s character, while a different but nonetheless enjoyable Franco-Spanish style of music can also be heard in Jules Massenet's *Don Quichotte*, Offenbach's *Los Habladores* and Maurice Ravel's *L'heure espagnole*.

Left France's leading composer of light opera, Jacques Offenbach, photographed in 1876.

Other operas by Bizet

Considering the huge success of *Carmen*, it is surprising that so many of Bizet's other works for the stage should have remained largely unknown to this day. All of his operas, though, contain music that is delightful, original, inventive and moving.

LA MAISON DU DOCTEUR
(The Doctor's House)

*Comic opera in **one act***
*Composed about **1855***
*First performed at **Texas University, United States, 1989***
Bizet's charming light comedy was greatly influenced by the Italian *buffo* style. The music has just a piano accompaniment (it was never scored for orchestra) and was quite possibly only ever intended for salon performance.

LE DOCTEUR MIRACLE
(Doctor Miracle)

*Operetta in **one act***
*First performed in **Paris, 1857***
This bubbly operetta was composed as an entry for a competition organized by Jacques Offenbach. Bizet came joint first with the talented composer Charles Lecocq and both works were performed eleven times at Offenbach's theatre. Bizet was only eighteen when he composed it but the work is typical of his well-mastered musical wit.

DON PROCOPIO

*Opera buffa in **two acts***
*Composed between **1858 and 59***
*First performed in **Monte Carlo, 1906***
Composed in Rome, Bizet's third opera is a sparkling opera buffa. The story (and indeed the musical style) is much the same as Donizetti's famous *Don Pasquale*. A young and beautiful girl feigns a strong will and gross extravagance to avoid being married to a rich old miser.

IVAN IV

*"Grand opera" in **five acts***
*Composed between **1862 and 1863***
*First performed (concert version with piano accompaniment only) in **Paris, 1943***
Much to Bizet's regret this opera was never performed during his lifetime. Regarded today as an uneven work, and thus rarely staged, the opera is based on the Russian story of Tsar Ivan, his love for the Caucasian Princess Marie, and his eventual thwarting of the evil conspirator, Yorloff.

LES PECHEURS DE PERLES
(The Pearl Fishers)

*Opera in **three acts***
*Libretto by **Eugène Cormon and Michel Carré***
*Original language **French***

Left A costume design for *Les pêcheurs de perles*.

First performed in **Paris, 1867**
Approximate length **120 minutes**

With probably the worst libretto Bizet ever set to music, the work nonetheless contains some light but magical music, especially in the second act. The plot concerns two rivals competing for the love of Catherine Glover, a sixteenth-century Scottish maiden. Too many misunderstandings send Catherine temporarily insane, but she is cured in the end by the successful Henry's glorious singing.

DJAMILEH

Opera in one act
Libretto by **Louis Gallet** *after* **Alfred de Musset**
Original language French
First performed in **Paris, 1872**
Approximate length **60 minutes**

In this short, beautiful and tuneful opera (and the composer's most sadly underrated work), Bizet sets to music the story of a slave girl, Djamileh, who is desperately in love with her Egyptian master, Haroun. He is a wanton fellow who spends money on gambling and procuring a new slave girl every month. When Djamileh's month comes to an end she longs to stay. In disguise and with the connivance of Haroun's tutor, Splendiano, she presents herself as the new slave girl. When Haroun discovers the truth he rejects her, but eventually, overcome by his feelings, he admits that he loves her and all ends happily.

First performed in **Paris, 1863**
Approximate length **105 minutes**

After *Carmen*, *Les pêcheurs de perles* is Bizet's most popular opera. One of the reasons for this is the justly famous pearl-fishers' duet "Au fond du temple saint" and the beautiful high tenor solo, "Je crois entendre encore." The tribal chief, Zurga, and his old friend Nadir are briefly reunited after their rival wooing of the fair priestess, Leïla. When the illicit affair between Nadir and Leïla is revealed, however, Zurga condemns them both to death. Zurga later discovers that Leïla saved his life many years ago, so he deliberately sets fire to the camp, enabling the young lovers to escape. He himself falls victim to the flames. The action is set in Ceylon (Sri Lanka).

LA JOLIE FILLE DE PERTH
(The Fair Maid of Perth)

Opera in four acts
Libretto by **Jules Adenis, Jules-Henri Vernoy** *and* **Marquis de Saint-Georges,** *freely adapted from Sir Walter Scott's*
The Fair Maid of Perth
Original language French

PUCCINI:
TOSCA

CD tracks 42 (timeline) and 43

Opera in *three acts*
Music by *Giacomo Puccini*
Libretto by *Giuseppe Giacosa* and *Luigi Illica*
after the play **La Tosca** by *Victorien Sardou*
Original language *Italian*
First performed in *Rome, 1900*
Approximate length *120 minutes*

Catherine Malfitano and Placido Domingo being filmed at dawn at the Castel Sant'Angelo in Rome for a production of Tosca that was broadcast live at the exact times and places envisaged by Puccini's librettists.

Tosca is one of the most dramatic and compelling operas ever written, which is why it has remained one of the most popular works of the entire repertoire since its premiere in Rome in 1900. It contains all the essential ingredients of love, death, violence, sex, corruption, power and loyalty, with a storyline of such burning intensity that the action in any production, however good or bad, moves along at a tremendous pace. Puccini's music is ingeniously suited to the plot – lush harmonies, rich orchestration and a plethora of sublime melodies combine to amplify the opera's themes of passionate love and loyalty, while the extraordinary vocal lines and growling sounds of double-bassoon and bass trombone echo the feelings of hysteria, fear and evil that bring the drama so vividly to life.

Summary of the plot

The action takes place over a period of twenty-four hours in Rome, 1800, in real locations that still exist. Act I is set in the beautiful church of Sant' Andrea della Valle, Act II in Scarpia's rooms at the Palazzo Farnese and the final tragic act takes place on the ramparts of the Castel Sant'Angelo. Scarpia, the dreaded police chief, is searching for an escaped prisoner. He rightly assumes that the painter, Mario Cavaradossi, knows something of the prisoner's whereabouts but cannot extract any information from him even under torture. Cavaradossi's lover, the singer Floria Tosca, is witness to the torture and eventually tells Scarpia where to find the prisoner in order to spare Cavaradossi any further pain. When Cavaradossi is dragged out, the lascivious Scarpia tells Tosca that her lover will be executed unless she is prepared to yield to his sexual demands. She finally agrees to his proposition provided he fakes the firing squad and guarantees safe conduct out of Rome for her and Cavaradossi. She finds herself unable to submit to Scarpia's desires, however, and instead she kills him with a knife. In the last act Tosca tells Cavaradossi to pretend to be dead after his mock execution. The shots ring out, and to her horror she discovers that Scarpia has double-crossed her: the bullets were real instead of blanks and Cavaradossi is dead. The curtain comes down as she throws herself over the ramparts of the Castel Sant'Angelo in a final gesture of hysterical operatic despair.

A brief history of the opera

Victorien Sardou's French play, *La Tosca*, was written in 1887, some thirteen years before the operatic premiere of *Tosca* in 1900, but the idea for the opera was first suggested to Puccini as early as 1890. His publisher, Giulio Ricordi, was keen to progress the project but because Puccini was fully occupied with two other operas, *Manon Lescaut* and *La Bohème*, Ricordi passed the idea on to the popular Italian composer, Alberto Franchetti. When Puccini eventually found time to resume his interest in *Tosca*, the idea was skilfully wrested from Franchetti. Puccini laboured hard to make *Tosca* as realistic as possible, consulting priests on the liturgy for the church scene in Act I. He even made a special trip to Rome to inspect the places where the action was set and to note the pitches of the bells at the Castel Sant'Angelo and St Peter's Basilica. The premiere on 12 July 1900 at the Teatro Costanzi was attacked by the critics (mainly for the libretto), but the public adored *Tosca* and performances of the opera spread like wildfire around the world.

DRAMATIS PERSONAE

Floria Tosca a celebrated singer . . . . soprano
Mario Cavaradossi a painter . . . . . . tenor
Baron Scarpia Chief of Police . . . . . baritone
Cesare Angelotti former consul
of the Roman Republic . . . . bass
A sacristan . . . . bass
Spoletta a police agent . . . . tenor
Sciarrone a gendarme . . . . bass
A jailer . . . . bass
A shepherd-boy . . . . alto

Choruses of soldiers, police agents, noblemen and women, townspeople and artisans

Setting Rome, June 1800

The exceptional soprano Maria Callas as Tosca. She can be heard singing "Vissi d'arte" from the opera on CD track 42.

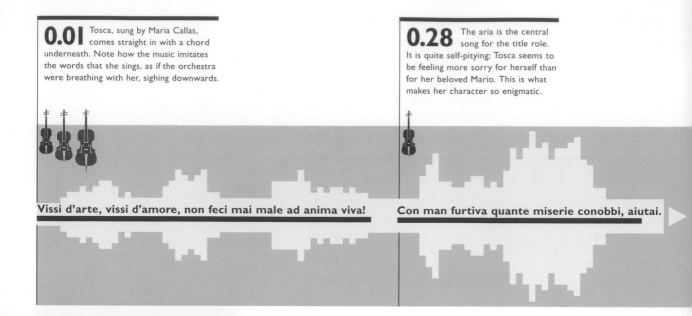

0.01 Tosca, sung by Maria Callas, comes straight in with a chord underneath. Note how the music imitates the words that she sings, as if the orchestra were breathing with her, sighing downwards.

0.28 The aria is the central song for the title role. It is quite self-pitying: Tosca seems to be feeling more sorry for herself than for her beloved Mario. This is what makes her character so enigmatic.

Vissi d'arte, vissi d'amore, non feci mai male ad anima viva!

Con man furtiva quante miserie conobbi, aiutai.

Leona Mitchell sings "Vissi d'arte" at the Sydney Opera House.

■ **Tosca**

Vissi d'arte, vissi d'amore,	I have lived for art and for love,
non feci mai male ad anima viva.	I have never harmed a living soul.
Con man furtiva	I have secretly helped so many of
quante miserie conobbi, aiutai.	the unlucky people I have known.
Sempre con fè sincera la mia	In sincere faith my prayers have
preghiera ai santi tabernacoli salì.	always risen to the holy tabernacles.
Sempre con fè sincera,	With sincere faith I have always put
diedi fiori agli altar.	flowers on the altars.

"Vissi d'arte" and other highlights

Tosca's Act II aria "Vissi d'arte, vissi d'amore" (I have lived for art and love: **CD track 42**, and see the "timeline" above) is often seen as the focal point of the whole opera. It is sung at a moment of great tension, when the tortured Cavaradossi has been carried off and Scarpia has offered Tosca a terrible choice: to submit to his lust or cause Cavaradossi's execution. Puccini himself felt that "Vissi d'arte" interrupted the flow of the drama and wanted to remove it from the opera. He may have been right about this, but as an aria it is both beautiful and usefully incisive at the point where it occurs. The aria is a prayer addressed directly to God. Tosca tells how decent she has been, how holy and honest, and bitterly laments the fate that God

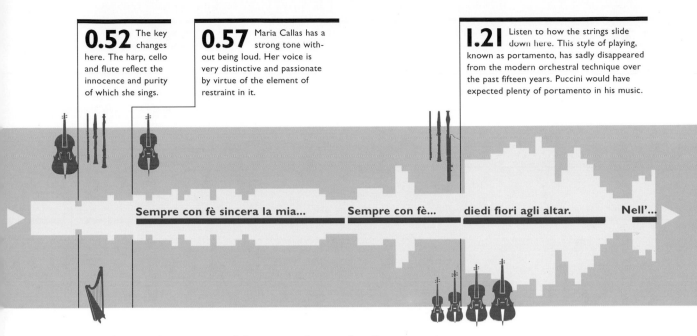

0.52 The key changes here. The harp, cello and flute reflect the innocence and purity of which she sings.

0.57 Maria Callas has a strong tone without being loud. Her voice is very distinctive and passionate by virtue of the element of restraint in it.

1.21 Listen to how the strings slide down here. This style of playing, known as portamento, has sadly disappeared from the modern orchestral technique over the past fifteen years. Puccini would have expected plenty of portamento in his music.

Sempre con fè sincera la mia...   Sempre con fè...   diedi fiori agli altar.   Nell'...

has thrown to her. In the context of the opera, the words tell us a great deal about the theatrical and desperate sides to her nature.

The opera is one great musical highlight after another, but among the most popular arias are Cavaradossi's bracing "Recondita armonia" (**CD track 43**) and the reflective "E lucevan le stelle" as he contemplates his imminent death. The three famous chords played as the curtain goes up represent Scarpia's evil and recur at key points throughout the opera.

The libretto and its origins

When Puccini first considered using *La Tosca* as the basis for an opera, he urged Ricordi to obtain permission from the playwright. Sardou refused, however, probably because Puccini was hardly known while Sardou enjoyed considerable fame across Europe as the writer of historical melodramas, particularly *Patrie!* (1869), *La haine* (1874) and *Fédora* (1882). By the time Puccini returned to the project, though, he was very well known, and Sardou now had no qualms about allowing the composer to base an opera on his work.

Cavaradossi's execution in Act III. Renzo Mongiardino designed the sets for this famous, long-running production of *Tosca* at the Royal Opera House in London.

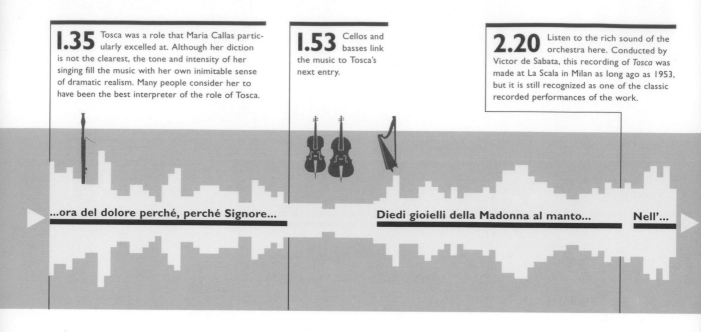

1.35 Tosca was a role that Maria Callas particularly excelled at. Although her diction is not the clearest, the tone and intensity of her singing fill the music with her own inimitable sense of dramatic realism. Many people consider her to have been the best interpreter of the role of Tosca.

1.53 Cellos and basses link the music to Tosca's next entry.

2.20 Listen to the rich sound of the orchestra here. Conducted by Victor de Sabata, this recording of *Tosca* was made at La Scala in Milan as long ago as 1953, but it is still recognized as one of the classic recorded performances of the work.

...ora del dolore perché, perché Signore...

Diedi gioielli della Madonna al manto...

Nell'...

Giuseppe Giacosa (1847-1906) and Luigi Illica (1857-1919) were given the task of simplifying Sardou's five-act play into a libretto suitable for a three-act opera. Illica planned the scenario and drafted the dialogue which he then gave to Giacosa to transcribe into polished verse. Sardou was apparently very pleased with the result; he once stated that the libretto was better than his original play. Giacosa and Illica collaborated on two of Puccini's other great successes: *La Bohème* and *Madama Butterfly*. Giacosa was the more established of the two, and his good nature and benign presence earned him his affectionate nickname of "the Buddha." After Giacosa's death, Puccini chose to collaborate with other librettists, to the lasting irritation of Illica.

Giacomo Puccini, who composed much of his music at the piano in his lakeside home at Torre del Lago.

The composer: Giacomo Puccini (1858–1924)

Puccini came from a long line of composers and musicians from the Tuscan town of Lucca. He won critical acclaim at the Milan Conservatoire for his orchestral piece *Capriccio Sinfonico* (1883), but it was not until he wrote his third opera, *Manon Lescaut*, ten years later, that he really found a personal voice

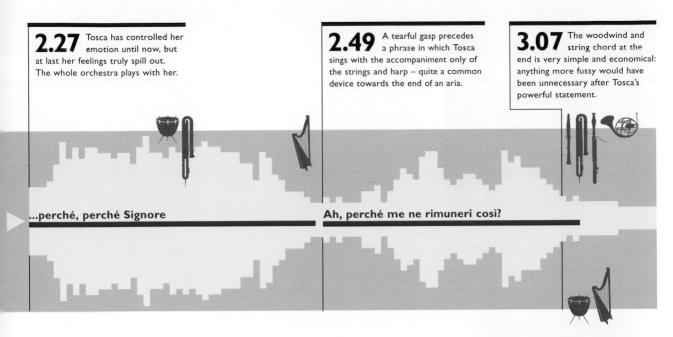

2.27 Tosca has controlled her emotion until now, but at last her feelings truly spill out. The whole orchestra plays with her.

2.49 A tearful gasp precedes a phrase in which Tosca sings with the accompaniment only of the strings and harp – quite a common device towards the end of an aria.

3.07 The woodwind and string chord at the end is very simple and economical: anything more fussy would have been unnecessary after Tosca's powerful statement.

...perché, perché Signore

Ah, perché me ne rimuneri così?

Nell'ora del dolore,	Now, in the hour of my pain,
perché, perché Signor,	why, my Lord,
perché me ne rimuneri così?	why do you repay me like this?
Diedi gioielli della Madonna al manto,	I have jewels for the cloak of Our Lady,
e diedi il canto agli astri,	I have offered my songs to the stars and
al ciel, che ne ridean più belli.	to heaven and made them more beautiful.
Nell'ora del dolore	In the hour of my pain,
perché, perché Signor,	why, my Lord,
ah, perché me ne rimuneri così?	why do you repay me like this?

and consequently a large following. He left long gaps between composing operas in which he revelled in each success and indulged his passion for hunting, shooting, motorcars and speed boats. His frequently turbulent married life was punctured by a scandal in which his wife, Elvira, wrongly accused him of having an affair with his maid. The matter ended with the maid's suicide and litigation between the composer and her parents. Puccini is often seen as a conservative composer, but if his harmonies and melodies were not exactly novel for their time, he nevertheless brought a new dramatic urgency and potent emotion into opera. His last opera, *Turandot*, was left unfinished at the time of his death and is most often heard today in a version completed by the younger composer, Franco Alfano.

Showing Tosca placing candles by the body of her victim, Scarpia, this poster for a 1900 production of the opera was considered quite shocking at the time.

Where to go next

If you enjoyed *Tosca*, the two operas Puccini wrote immediately before and after it, *La Bohème* and *Madama Butterfly*, are the obvious places to look next. All three operas are distinguished by music that is tuneful, opulent and vehemently emotional. Other fascinating works of the Italian "verismo" school include Umberto Giordano's *Fedora* and *Andrea Chénier*, Pietro Mascagni's *Cavalleria rusticana* and *Iris*, Alfredo Catalani's *La Wally* and Ruggiero Leoncavallo's *I pagliacci*.

Left Butterfly sits with her son and her maid Suzuki (left) in the last act of *Madama Butterfly* in a production by English National Opera.

Other operas by Puccini

Puccini was a hugely successful composer, and only his second major opera, *Edgar*, is not regularly performed today. Of his shorter rarities, *La rondine* (The Swallow) and the comedy, *Gianni Schicchi,* are both extraordinary.

MANON LESCAUT

Opera in four acts
*Libretto by **Luigi Illica, Giuseppe Giacosa,***
Giulio Ricordi, Marco Prago** and **Domenico Oliva
*after **Abbé Prevost's** **L'Histoire du Chevalier des***
Grieux et de Manon Lescaut
*Original language **Italian***
*First performed in **Turin, 1893***
*Approximate length **120 minutes***

In Puccini's third opera and first great success, Manon falls in love with a poor young aristocrat, des Grieux, but leaves him to become the mistress of the wealthy Geronte. When she meets des Grieux again some time later, she elopes with him, taking the jewels that Geronte had given her. Geronte has them arrested, however, and Manon is deported to Louisiana. Des Grieux follows her there, but she dies of exhaustion in his arms. Puccini truly found his musical voice with this opera, which is full of memorable tunes and stirring passions.

LA BOHÈME (Bohemian Life)

Opera in four acts
*Libretto by **Luigi Illica, Giuseppe Giacosa** after **Henri***
Murger's novel, **Scènes de la vie de bohème**

*Original language **Italian***
*First performed in **Turin, 1896***
*Approximate length **105 minutes***

La Bohème is probably the most popular opera in the entire repertoire. Its success is based on its beautiful tunes, its tight and relevant drama and sublime juxtaposition of frivolous merriment and painful tragedy. Rodolfo, a penniless poet sharing a Parisian garret with artistic friends, is in love with the consumptive seamstress, Mimì. After a brief separation they are reunited, only for Mimì to die in his arms, shivering from illness and cold.

MADAMA BUTTERFLY

Opera in three acts
*Libretto by **Luigi Illica** and **Giuseppe Giacosa** after a play*
*by **David Belasco***
*Original language **Italian***
*First performed in **Milan, 1904***
*Approximate length **120 minutes***

Based on a supposedly true story, Puccini's Japanese opera is rich with orientally inspired music. An American naval officer, Lieutenant Pinkerton, marries a geisha girl (Cio-Cio-San, known as Butterfly) while his ship is docked in a Japanese port. He abandons her and returns to America, but she struggles on, rejected by her family, bearing him a child and waiting in eager and constant anticipation of his return. When he does eventually come back he brings with him his new American wife. Cio-Cio-San is devastated and stabs herself, leaving the guilt-ridden Pinkerton to care for their three-year-old son.

LA FANCIULLA DEL WEST
(The Girl of the Golden West)

Opera in three acts
Original language Italian
Libretto by Carlo Zangarini and Guelfo Civinini after David Belasco's play
First performed in New York, 1910
Approximate length 120 minutes

Set in the cowboy days of the Wild West, Minnie, a saloon mistress, falls in love with a bandit, Dick Johnson, and twice saves his life: when the Sheriff tries to arrest him and when goldminers try to hang him. Puccini's music is terser and less yielding than in his other operas, and this work has consequently never been quite as popular.

TURANDOT

Opera in three acts
Original language Italian
Libretto by Renato Simoni and Giuseppe Adami after the play by Carlo Gozzi
First performed in Milan, 1926
Approximate length 105 minutes

Puccini's last opera was left unfinished at the time of his death. The Emperor promises the hand in marriage of his daughter, the icy Princess Turandot, to any man who can solve three riddles – but warns that a wrong answer is punishable by summary execution. Although the brave Calaf answers all the questions correctly, Turandot will not consent to marry him. Calaf agrees to die for her if she can find out his name before dawn. Turandot tortures his loyal servant, Liù, but to no avail (Liù kills herself). In the end Calaf reveals his name to her, but by now he has managed to melt her icy heart and the story ends happily. The opera's most famous highlight is the rousing aria "Nessun dorma," popularized by the tenor Luciano Pavarotti.

Left A street scene from *La fanciulla del West*, staged at the Metropolitan Opera House in New York. **Below** A magnificent production of Puccini's last opera, *Turandot*, at the Verona Arena in Italy.

CHAPTER SIX

A Guide to 50 Further Essential Operas

BELA BARTOK (1881–1945)
DUKE BLUEBEARD'S CASTLE

Opera in **one act** *to a Hungarian libretto by* **Béla Balázs**
after a fairy tale by **Charles Perrault**
First performed in **Budapest, 1918**
Approximate length **60 minutes**

Bartók's low, dark music is perfect for this weird and horrific tale. Judith has come to live in the damp castle of her new husband, Duke Bluebeard. Her curiosity is such that she insists on opening seven locked doors. Behind each she finds clues to his violent past. The seventh door reveals three of Bluebeard's previous wives. Judith reluctantly joins them, leaving Bluebeard alone once more.

LUDWIG VAN BEETHOVEN (1770–1827)
FIDELIO

Opera in **two acts** *to a German libretto by* **Joseph von Sonnleithner** *and* **George Friedrich Treitschke**
First performed in **Vienna, 1805** *(final version* **1814)**
Approximate length **135 minutes**

Beethoven's only opera is hard to stage, and some would argue that it is really an extended symphony that works

Opposite Placido Domingo and Agnes Baltsa in Offenbach's
Les contes d'Hoffmann. **Insets, clockwise from top left** Scenes
from J. Strauss's *Die Fledermaus*, Tchaikovsky's *Eugene Onegin*,
R. Strauss's *Elektra* and Leoncavallo's *I pagliacci*.

better on the concert platform than in the opera house. Nobody would disagree, however, that the opera contains some of the finest and most uplifting music Beethoven ever composed. Leonore, dressed as a man and calling herself Fidelio, enters the prison service in order to free her unjustly imprisoned husband, Florestan. The opera contains elements of comedy and deals with issues of conjugal loyalty, love and liberty with impassioned directness. It is one of the most exhilarating operas ever written.

VINCENZO BELLINI (1801–35)
NORMA

Opera in **two acts** *to an Italian libretto by* **Felice Romani**
after a drama by **L.A. Soumet**
First performed in **Milan, 1831**
Approximate length **180 minutes**

For those particularly thrilled by the virtuoso sound of a coloratura soprano, *Norma* is one of the most exciting operas of its kind. The challenging role has proved a perfect vehicle for many great sopranos, notably Joan Sutherland, Maria Callas and Montserrat Caballé. The priestess Norma, despairing of ever winning back her disaffected lover, the Roman proconsul Pollione, confesses her love and is condemned to death. Racked with guilt and remorse, Pollione joins her on the funeral pyre. The opera contains the much-loved aria, "Casta diva" (**CD track 26**).

Above left Faye Robinson in Bellini's *I Puritani* at New York City Opera. *Above right* A lavish production of Berlioz's epic *Les Troyens* at the Royal Opera House in London.

I PURITANI (The Puritans)

Opera in **three acts** *to an Italian libretto by* **Carlo Pepoli**
First performed in **Paris, 1835**
Approximate length **150 minutes**

Bellini's last opera combines all the most dramatic, tuneful and virtuosic elements of his work that have made him such a popular Romantic composer. To save Queen Henrietta from execution during the English Civil War, Arthur Talbot disguises her in the wedding dress of his fiancée, Elvira, and whisks her from the castle. Elvira sees them leave and, believing herself betrayed, goes mad. When Arthur returns, however, her sanity is restored.

ALBAN BERG (1885–1935)
WOZZECK

Opera in **three acts** *to a German libretto by* **Berg** *after* **Georg Büchner's** *play,* **Woyzeck**
First performed in **Berlin, 1925**
Approximate length **90 minutes**

Berg takes the psychological angle of German expressionism to its limits in his only completed opera. The strange music, by turns sensuous and lyrical, barbaric and dissonant, echoes the psychotic nightmare of Wozzeck, an impoverished soldier who supports his lover, Marie, by submitting to the experiments of a mad doctor. When Wozzeck discovers her with the coarse Drum Major, he stabs her and drowns himself in a nearby pond – an ugly scenario, but a gripping opera.

HECTOR BERLIOZ (1803–69)
LES TROYENS (The Trojans)

Opera in **five acts** *to a French libretto by* **Berlioz** *after* **Virgil's** Aeneid
First performed in **Paris, 1863** *(acts III–V only);*
complete version **Karlsruhe, 1890**
Approximate length **225 minutes**

Berlioz considered *Les Troyens* to be his masterpiece and bitterly regretted the fact that it was never performed in its entirety during his lifetime. In effect *Les Troyens* is two operas ingeniously conceived as one. In the first part, *La Prise de Troie* (Acts I–II), Cassandra foresees the sacking of Troy, but no one believes her. When the Greek soldiers arrive, she and other brave Trojan women leap to their deaths. In the second part, *Les Troyens à Carthage*, Aeneas leads the survivors to found a new Trojan city in Italy, but is delayed *en route* by his love affair with the Carthaginian queen, Dido. When duty compels Aeneas to leave her shores, Dido kills herself. It is a long opera full of colour, drama, grandeur and intimacy.

ALEKSANDR BORODIN (1833–87)
PRINCE IGOR

*Opera in **four acts** to a Russian libretto by **Borodin***
after an anonymous twelfth-century work
*First performed in **St Petersburg, 1890***
*Approximate length **210 minutes***

A sprawling epic that has come to be seen as one of the central pieces of nationalist Russian "grand opera," *Prince Igor* is best known for the beautiful Polovtsian dances, the most famous of which has found its way into the Broadway musical, *Kismet*. The opera also contains other themes that derive from Russian folk traditions. Igor and his son Vladimir are imprisoned by the Tartar ruler Khan Kontchak. Vladimir falls in love with Kontchak's daughter, however, and stays behind after his father's escape.

BENJAMIN BRITTEN (1913–76)
PETER GRIMES

*Opera in **three acts** to an English libretto by **Montagu Slater***
*after **George Crabbe's** poem, **The Borough***
*First performed in **London, 1945***
*Approximate length **135 minutes***

Peter Grimes established Britten's international reputation as soon as it was premiered in 1945. The theme of an individual ostracized by a hostile local community was developed by Britten in most of his later operas. Grimes, a lonely Suffolk fisherman, is hounded by the villagers and driven to suicide when two of his apprentices die in accidental circumstances. The music is not difficult to enjoy, the characters are extraordinarily vivid and the opera succeeds thanks to the strength of its mood.

BILLY BUDD

*Opera in **four acts** to an English libretto by **E.M. Forster***
*and **Eric Crozier** after **Herman Melville's** eponymous novel*
*First performed in **London, 1951***
*Approximate length **165 minutes***

Billy Budd is unusual in that it employs an all-male cast. The awesome power of Britten's music, amplified by a large and colourful orchestra, paints a terrifying scene of life on board a warship in 1797. Billy Budd, an amiable novice, is driven to distraction by the evil machinations of the officer Claggart. Stammering to defend himself from an unfounded allegation of mutiny, he strikes out at Claggart and accidentally kills him. Billy is sentenced to death. The whole shattering scenario is seen through the eyes of the humane but weak-minded Captain Vere.

CLAUDE DEBUSSY (1862–1918)
PELLEAS ET MELISANDE

*Opera in **five acts** to a French libretto taken from*
*the play by **Maurice Maeterlinck***
*First performed in **Paris, 1902***
*Approximate length **150 minutes***

This most haunting and atmospheric of operas centres on the mysteriously beautiful figure of Mélisande. Lost in a wood, she is rescued by Prince Golaud, who takes her to his castle and marries her; but the castle is dark and gloomy and she falls in love with his brother, Pelléas. Golaud is suspicious and eventually slays his brother in a fit of jealousy. The quiet Mélisande dies in childbirth. The setting is that of a medieval fairy-tale castle; the music is dark and slow, but exquisitely beautiful throughout.

Below Golaud (Willard White), Mélisande (Cathryn Pope) and Arkel (John Connell) in a scene from *Pelléas et Mélisande*.

GAETANO DONIZETTI (1797–1848)
L'ELISIR D'AMORE (The Elixir of Love)
Opera in two acts to an Italian libretto by Felice Romani
First performed in Milan, 1832
Approximate length 120 minutes

In this ever-popular comedy, which brims with robust and enchanting melodies, the clumsy peasant Nemorino is tricked into drinking wine in the belief that it is a magic love-potion. His drunken behaviour gives his intended, Adina, the impression that he no longer cares for her. True to the form of traditional farce, everything ends happily with Adina and Nemorino celebrating their union in the final scene. "Una furtiva lagrima" is a moving aria that has become an expressive showpiece popular with many leading tenors. Donizetti's energetic, inspired music easily makes up for the frivolous plot. When the opera is well acted, Nemorino's drunken scenes can be extremely funny.

LUCIA DI LAMMERMOOR
Opera in three acts to an Italian libretto by Salvatore Cammarano after Sir Walter Scott's novel, **The Bride of Lammermoor**
First performed in Naples, 1835
Approximate length 150 minutes

The combination of words and music are particularly adroit at portraying madness, but perhaps the most famous of all operatic mad scenes comes from *Lucia*. The opera is also memorable for a string of sturdy melodies and a terrifically invigorating sextet. Deceived into believing her lover (Edgardo) unfaithful and forced by her brother into a political marriage, Lucia is driven mad, kills her husband and then herself. When Edgardo later returns from France and discovers what has happened he stabs himself. Lucia is one of the most difficult coloratura roles.

Above The soprano June Anderson as Lucia in Donizetti's *Lucia di Lammermoor* at the Metropolitan Opera House, New York.

DON PASQUALE
Opera in three acts to an Italian libretto by Giovanni Ruffini and Donizetti
First performed in Milan, 1843
Approximate length 120 minutes

The basis of Donizetti's wittiest opera is a trick. Grumpy Don Pasquale threatens to disinherit his nephew, Ernesto, if he dares to marry Norina. Meanwhile, Pasquale is making it known that he himself would like to take a wife. Norina thus poses as a prospective bride for Pasquale, but makes life so disagreeable for him that by the end he agrees to anything Ernesto and Norina request of him. The patter song "Cheti, cheti, immantinente" between Don Pasquale and his friend, Doctor Malatesta, and Ernesto's wistful "Cercherò lontana terra" are particular favourites with most audiences.

ANTONIN DVORAK (1841–1904)
RUSALKA
Opera in three acts to a Czech libretto by Jaroslav Kvapil after Friedrich Fouqué's fairy tale, **Undine**
First performed in Prague, 1901
Approximate length 180 minutes

Sadly, Dvořák's nine operas are very rarely performed outside the Czech Republic, but *Rusalka*, the most famous and most passionate, is typical of all of them in its melodic charm. Rusalka, a water nymph, makes a deal with a witch that she might become human and marry a prince. One of the conditions imposed on her is that she should remain silent, but this bores the prince who turns instead to a foreign princess. Rusalka is transformed into a will-o'-the-wisp and the prince, regretting his infidelities, kisses her, knowing the kiss will kill him.

GEORGE GERSHWIN (1898–1937)
PORGY AND BESS
Opera in three acts to an English libretto by Ira Gershwin and Du Bose Heyward after Dorothy and Du Bose Heyward's play, **Porgy**

Below Cab Calloway as Sportin' Life, William Warfield as Porgy and Urlee Leandros as Bess in Gershwin's *Porgy and Bess*. *Right* A scene from Philip Glass's opera *Akhnaten*.

*First performed in **Boston, 1935***
*Approximate length **180 minutes***

Porgy and Bess comes close at times to the genre of Broadway musical, but the vocal passions, seriousness and length of the work qualify it as an opera. Set in the black community of a South Carolina tenement block, Bess chooses to leave her violent boyfriend (Crown) and start an honest life with the cripple Porgy. Things go wrong when Porgy is charged with murder and Bess takes drugs and runs off to New York. "Summertime," "It ain't necessarily so" and "I got plenty of nuttin'" are hit songs from Gershwin's only opera.

UMBERTO GIORDANO (1867–1948)
ANDREA CHENIER

*Opera in **four acts** to an Italian libretto by **Luigi Illica***
*First performed in **Milan, 1896***
*Approximate length **135 minutes***

Andrea Chénier is a classic work of Italian *verismo*, full of hot-blooded passion and surging romantic music. The action takes place during the French Revolution, when Chénier – a poet – is condemned to death by the new revolutionary leader, Gérard. Gérard's main motive is that both he and Chénier are in love with Maddalena. It is not until Gérard realizes the full, self-sacrificing extent of Maddalena's love for Chénier that he repents; but his attempts to rescue the poet from execution are all too late. Maddalena enters the prison and substitutes herself for another prisoner so that she can die with Chénier.

PHILIP GLASS (1937–)
AKHNATEN

*Opera in **three acts** to an English libretto assembled by Glass from **ancient Egyptian, Akkadian** and **biblical Hebrew** sources*
*First performed in **Stuttgart, 1984***
*Approximate length **135 minutes***

One of the great popular modern operas. Philip Glass's mesmerizing and richly atmospheric minimalist music poetically reflects a series of episodes in the life of the Egyptian pharaoh, Akhnaten. Akhnaten eschews tradition by announcing his belief in a single god. He builds a city to his god and withdraws into it, but his pantheistic people overthrow him and revert to the old order. Akhnaten and his family brood among the ruins of his city before joining their own funeral procession.

CHRISTOPH WILLIBALD VON GLUCK (1714–87)
ORFEO ED EURIDICE

*Opera in three acts to an Italian libretto by Ranieri
de' Calzabigi; the libretto was later translated into French
by Pierre-Louis Moline and entitled Orphée et Eurydice*
*First performed in Vienna, 1762; French revised
version Paris, 1774*
Approximate length 115 minutes

In the clearest, cleanest and most directly emotional
terms, Gluck unfolds the famous story of Orpheus and
his descent to the Underworld in the hope of retrieving
his beloved wife Euridice, who has died from a snake bite.
Orpheus's mourning informs the atmosphere of the
whole opera and his famous aria "Che farò senza
Euridice" (What can I do without Euridice?) is regarded
by many as one of the most moving moments in Classical
opera and a vindication of Gluck's theory that music in a
major key can be used to express grief.

IPHIGENIE EN AULIDE

*Opera in three acts to a French libretto by
Bailli Leblanc du Roullet*
First performed in Paris, 1774
Approximate length 150 minutes

The two Gluck operas based on the mythical Greek
figure of Iphigenia (*Iphigénie en Aulide* and *Iphigénie en
Tauride*) are both compelling works. In the first, Iphigenia
is summoned to Aulis by her father, Agamemnon, who
deceives her into believing she is to be married to Achilles.
In fact he intends to sacrifice her to secure safe passage
for the Greeks on their journey to Troy. When his plot
is discovered, a violent quarrel erupts between Achilles
and Agamemnon, even though Iphigenia has agreed to
be sacrificed. The gods are so impressed by human
behaviour, however, that the Greeks are permitted to sail
for Troy without making any sacrifice at all. This was the
first of seven operas Gluck composed for Paris.

ALCESTE

*Opera in three acts to an Italian libretto by
Ranieri de' Calzabigi, later translated into French
by Bailli Leblanc du Roullet*

Above Alceste (Janet Baker) and Admète (Robert Tear) in
a production of Gluck's masterful opera *Alceste* at the Royal
Opera House in London.

*First performed in Vienna, 1767;
French version Paris, 1776*
Approximate length 135 minutes

In Gluck's famous preface to *Alceste*, he laid down new
principles for opera, promising in essence a greater range
of expression and less adherence to old–fashioned
formality. The opera itself is a masterpiece of dramatic
characterization. Alceste agrees with the gods to lay down
her life to spare that of her husband, Admète, who is
suffering from a serious illness. When he discovers her
promise, he offers to die with her. The god Apollo is so
moved by their displays of conjugal loyalty, however, that
he allows them both to live.

CHARLES-FRANCOIS GOUNOD (1818–93)
FAUST

*Opera in five acts to a French libretto by Jules Barbier
and Michel Carré after Goethe's poem*
First performed in Paris, 1859
Approximate length 210 minutes

At first Gounod's *Faust* was considered a difficult opera
but now it is widely regarded as his best and most successful work. The story follows the familiar Faust legend.
Faust enters into a deal with the diabolic Méphistophélès

in which he exchanges his soul for eternal youth and the love of Marguerite. When Faust abandons Marguerite and slays her brother Valentin in a duel, she goes mad and kills their child. Only then is Faust repentant, but his remorse is too late. Angels lift Marguerite to heaven while Méphistophélès drags Faust down to hell.

ROMEO ET JULIETTE
Opera in five acts to a French libretto by Jules Barbier and Michel Carré after Shakespeare's play
First performed in Paris, 1867
Approximate length 195 minutes
Brilliantly orchestrated and richly romantic, Gounod's work is by far the most successful adaptation of Shakespeare's poignant Veronese tragedy for the operatic stage. It is also unusual in that it contains four great duets for the title characters. The story by and large follows Shakespeare's work except that the two lovers are briefly united for one final duet in the tomb scene, whereas in the original play Juliet awakes only after Romeo has killed himself.

GEORGE FRIDERIC HANDEL (1685–1759)
ORLANDO
Opera in three acts to an Italian libretto by Grazio Braccioli after Ludovico Ariosto's Orlando Furioso
First performed in London, 1733
Approximate length 180 minutes
Handel composed some forty operas and not many of them fall below his extraordinary high levels of excellence. The orchestration in *Orlando* is superb, proving Handel to be the most inventive of all Baroque opera composers. The opera centres on the frustrated jealous rages of Orlando (Furioso), and his hopeless love for Angelica, which lead eventually to his madness and contemplations of suicide. The mad scene in this opera is exceptional. The title role has been interpreted this century by both mezzo-sopranos (such as Marilyn Horne) and countertenors (such as James Bowman).

ENGELBERT HUMPERDINCK (1854–1921)
HANSEL UND GRETEL
Opera in three acts to a German libretto by Adelheid Wette after the Grimms' fairy tale
First performed in Weimar, 1893
Approximate length 120 minutes
Humperdinck's luscious score made *Hänsel und Gretel* one of the most popular operas of its time. Even now it is a regular Christmas treat for children all over Germany. The familiar tale of Hansel and Gretel's escapades into the woods and their encounter with the wicked witch in her candy house is set to music of the rarest beauty. It can be enjoyed both as a sophisticated adult psychological drama and as a simple fairy tale.

Left Roberto Alagna and Leontina Vaduva in Gounod's *Roméo et Juliette*. **Below** The witch imprisons Hansel in Humperdinck's *Hänsel und Gretel* at the Metropolitan Opera House, New York.

LEOS JANACEK (1854–1928)
JENUFA

*Opera in **three acts** to a Czech libretto by* **Janáček**
after a play by Gabriela Preissova
*First performed in **Brno**, 1904*
*Approximate length **120 minutes***

Janáček's first successful opera centres on the uncontrolled passions and prejudices of an isolated Czech village, with music that is brazen, powerful and perfectly suited to the horrific scenario. Jenůfa is made pregnant by the drunken Steva; his brother loves her but slashes her face in a jealous rage. Now too ugly for Steva, she is forced to give birth in secret. To save the family name Jenůfa's stepmother drowns the baby in the icy river while Jenůfa is asleep.

KATA KABANOVA

*Opera in **three acts** to a Czech libretto by* **Janáček**
*after **Aleksandr Ostrovsky's** play,* **The Storm**
*First performed in **Brno**, 1921*
*Approximate length **105 minutes***

Janáček's most intense, probing psychological drama is brilliantly brought to life by difficult, yet sympathetic and perceptive music. Káťa's life is made miserable by her interfering mother-in-law and depressing husband. Her uncontrollable love for Boris culminates in a meeting by the garden gate while her husband is out. When he returns she confesses, and in the uproar that follows Boris is banished and Káťa, overwhelmed with despair, throws herself into the freezing River Volga. Janáček was approaching seventy when this opera was first performed.

Above left Jenůfa, her baby and step-mother in Janáček's *Jenůfa* at the Metropolitan Opera House, New York. *Above right* A scene from Janáček's *The Cunning Little Vixen* at Châtelet in Paris.

THE CUNNING LITTLE VIXEN

*Opera in **three acts** to a Czech libretto by* **Janáček** *after*
Rudolf Tesnohlidek's** verses for drawings by **Stanislav Lolek
*First performed in **Brno**, 1924*
*Approximate length **90 minutes***

To compose an opera in which the title character and most of the supporting cast are animals might seem a risky venture, but Janáček succeeded in producing a work that was at once comic, disturbingly moving and invigorating. The vixen, at first a pet, bites off the heads of all the chickens and escapes captivity. She then marries the Fox, but is finally shot by a poacher. Animal scenes are interspersed with scenes between the poacher, the forester and other humans. Janáček's music is as vibrant and resourceful as ever, endowing even the animal parts with strongly defined characters.

RUGGIERO LEONCAVALLO (1857–1919)
I PAGLIACCI (Clowns)

*Opera with a **prologue** and **two acts** to an Italian*
*libretto by **Leoncavallo***
*First performed in **Milan**, 1892*
*Approximate length **60 minutes***

I pagliacci is so often performed with *Cavalleria rusticana* (*see opposite*) that the two are often referred to as "Cav and Pag." They are both immediate and vibrant operas that make a strong impact on the emotions. *Cavalleria* was the first of the two, and Leoncavallo attempted to create the same atmosphere of *verismo* in his *I pagliacci*. While performing a play, Canio murders his wife and her lover, after he is told of their affair by the hunchback clown, Tonio.

PIETRO MASCAGNI (1863–1945)
CAVALLERIA RUSTICANA (Rustic Chivalry)

*Opera in **one act** to an Italian libretto by **Giovanni Targioni-Tozzetti** and **Guido Menasci** after **Giovanni Verga***
*First performed in **Rome, 1890***
*Approximate length **75 minutes***

Mascagni never managed to repeat the success of *Cavalleria* (his first opera), which is now seen as one of the founding works of the Italian *verismo* school. It is a tuneful and passionate work about adultery and revenge in a small Sicilian village. The beautiful orchestral intermezzo is often performed as a separate concert work for orchestra. The opera also includes Turiddu's melancholic opening melody and a brilliant drinking song towards the end.

JULES MASSENET (1842–1912)
MANON

*Opera in **five acts** to a French libretto by **Henri Meilhac** and **Philippe Gille** after **Abbé Prévost's** novel, **Histoire du chevalier des Grieux et de Manon Lescaut***
*First performed in **Paris, 1884***
*Approximate length **150 minutes***

Massenet's lush, romantic style and unerring ability to compose a big tune just when it is needed are perfectly matched to the mood and tragic plot of Abbé Prévost's *Manon Lescaut*. Des Grieux's father has him abducted because he disapproves of his liaison with the "immoral" Manon. Manon leads a disreputable life of luxury, and when she and des Grieux are later arrested in a casino she is sentenced to deportation as a prostitute. Des Grieux's attempt to rescue her on the road to Le Havre is ineffectual and she dies in his arms.

Below Manon (Faith Esham) faces the chorus in Act III of Massenet's tragedy, *Manon*, produced at New York City Opera.

WERTHER

*Opera in **four acts** to a French libretto by **Edouard Blau**, **Paul Milliet** and **Georges Hartmann** after **Goethe's** novel, **Die Leiden des jungen Werthers** (The sorrows of Young Werther)*
*First performed in **Vienna, 1892***
*Approximate length **150 minutes***

Goethe's story of Werther was guaranteed to appeal to a romantic, nineteenth-century opera composer like Massenet. It is the story of an obsession. The melancholy young Werther is desperately in love with Charlotte, but she is promised to Albert, whom she marries in Werther's absence. Only after Werther has fatally shot himself does Charlotte admit to having loved him all along. *Werther* has been Massenet's most celebrated work for more than a century; the title role has been sung over the years by such masterly interpreters as Tito Schipa, Nicolai Gedda, Alfredo Kraus, José Carreras and Placido Domingo.

Top José Carreras and Maria Ewing embrace in a scene from Massenet's tragic opera, *Werther*, at San Francisco Opera House. **Above** Jean Rigby as Penelope (left) in Monteverdi's *Il ritorno d'Ulisse in patria*, staged by English National Opera, London.

CLAUDIO MONTEVERDI (1567–1643)
L'ORFEO

*Opera in **five acts** to an Italian libretto by **Alessandro Striggio***
*First performed in **Mantua, 1607***
*Approximate length **105 minutes***

The earliest opera that still appears regularly on the modern opera stage, *L'Orfeo* is also one of the most stirring of all the many operatic settings of the Orpheus legend. Orpheus descends to Hades to retrieve his wife, Euridice, from the dead. His desperate singing lulls the ferryman Charon to sleep, enabling him to punt himself over the River Styx. But when he eventually finds Euridice he breaks the rules by looking back at her, and she disappears once again. In this version of the story Apollo takes pity and Orpheus and Euridice are reunited in immortality. In Monteverdi's day operas were expected to have happy endings. The opera is bursting with vigour and almost folk-like tunes.

IL RITORNO D'ULISSE IN PATRIA
(The Return of Ulysses)

*Opera in **five acts** to an Italian libretto by **Giacomo Badoaro***
*First performed in **Venice, 1640***
*Approximate length **180 minutes***

A more serious, perhaps less tuneful opera than *L'Orfeo*, composed over thirty years later, but no less moving at key points. Penelope has been waiting twenty years for her roving husband Ulysses to return. She has remained faithful to him despite offers from many suitors. When Ulysses does eventually return, he disguises himself as a beggar, but as the only person among Penelope's admirers to be able to string Ulysses' bow, he wins a competition, slays all Penelope's suitors and is happily reunited with his patient wife. Monteverdi's first opera for Venice was a huge success in the composer's lifetime.

JACQUES OFFENBACH (1819–80)
LES CONTES D'HOFFMANN
(The Tales of Hoffmann)

*Opera with a **prologue, three acts** and an **epilogue**, to a French libretto by **Jules Barbier** and **Michel Carré** after three stories by **E.T.A. Hoffmann***

Left The marionette Nicklausse behind a veil in a scene from Act I of *Les Contes d'Hoffmann*, produced at the Théâtre du Châtelet in Paris. *Below* Galina Gorchakova as the disturbed heroine, Renata, in Prokofiev's dark opera *The Fiery Angel*, performed at the Kirov Opera in St Petersburg.

*First performed in **Paris**, 1881*
*Approximate length **170 minutes***

Offenbach left his last opera unfinished at his death and there has been much scholarly debate about the correct way of performing it. It is less frivolous than any of his operettas and, following more in the tradition of Hoffmann's writing, it is a romantic fantasy, at times grotesque but always compelling. At an inn, Hoffmann tells of his three lovers, who transpire to be different facets of the same girl, Stella. The first story is about a doll named Olympia who is destroyed by the man who created her, Coppélius, the second tells the tale of Antonia, who is forced by an evil doctor to sing herself to death; and the last tale concerns the Venetian courtesan Giulietta, who turns out to be faithless. At the end of the opera, Stella leaves the inn in the arms of another man, Lindorf. The luxuriant "Barcarole" from Act IV is the opera's most celebrated moment.

JOHN PEPUSCH (1667–1752)
THE BEGGAR'S OPERA

*Opera in **three acts**, arranged and partially composed*
*to an English libretto by **John Gay***
*First performed in **London**, 1728*
*Approximate length **180 minutes***

John Gay's inspired work in devising and putting together *The Beggar's Opera* using famous tunes by other composers (notably Handel, Purcell and Bononcini) led to a whole new genre of ballad opera that eventually spawned the German *singspiel*, French comic opera and the Anglo-American musical. The plot, about a lowlife highwayman, involves plenty of contemporary satire (some of which is hard to appreciate now), and an abundance of fine tunes and racy stories makes this a thoroughly enjoyable opera.

SERGEI PROKOFIEV (1891–1953)
THE FIERY ANGEL

*Opera in **five acts** to a Russian libretto by **Prokofiev** after*
Valery Bryusov's novel of the same name
*First performed (in concert version) in **Paris**, 1954*
*Approximate length **120 minutes***

A terrifying work, made especially so by Prokofiev's powerful, brooding music and the deeply disturbing plot. The opera was composed in 1927 but the Soviet authorities deemed it unsuitable and it was never staged in Prokofiev's lifetime. Ruprecht falls in love with the hysterical Renata, who is obsessed by visions of her ex-lover, Count Heinrich. Ruprecht helps Renata to find Heinrich, but the two men end up fighting a duel in which Ruprecht is wounded. Renata eventually leaves Ruprecht and enters a convent in a state of remorse about her madness and the problems it has caused; but when the nuns become possessed by evil spirits, Renata, blamed for the chaos, is sentenced to death by the Grand Inquisitor.

JEAN-PHILIPPE RAMEAU (1683–1764)
LES INDES GALANTES (Gallantry in the Indies)

*Opera with a **prologue** and **four entrées** to a French*
*libretto by **Louis Fuzelier***
*First performed (with 2 entrées) in **Paris, 1735***
*Approximate length **150 minutes***

This perfect example of Rameau's imaginative balletic opera style proved to be the greatest success of the composer's life. Not often performed outside France, *Les Indes galantes* needs to be given the lavish stage treatment that it had when it was first produced. Of the four love stories, each in an exotic setting (Turkey, Peru, Persia and America), perhaps the most spectacular is the second, in which a megalomaniacal Inca High Priest provokes a volcanic eruption because of his frustrated sexual jealousy.

CAMILLE SAINT-SAENS (1835–1921)
SAMSON ET DALILA

*Opera in **three acts** to a French libretto by*
Ferdinand Lemaire** after the **Old Testament
*First performed in **Weimar, 1877***
*Approximate length **130 minutes***

True to the most lavish traditions of French "grand opera," Saint-Saëns' *Samson* offers a terrific feast of ballet, chorus and special effects, but at its heart is the romantic but ultimately fatal love that Samson, the Israelite leader, feels for the Philistine seductress Dalila. Samson is charmed by Dalila into revealing the source of his super-human strength, his hair, which she cuts off. Thus betrayed, Samson is captured by the Philistines and blinded. His prayers are answered with strength enough to destroy the Temple of Dagon, killing his adversaries and himself.

DMITRI SHOSTAKOVICH (1906–75)
LADY MACBETH OF MTSENSK

*Opera in **four acts** to a Russian libretto by **Alexander***
Preis** and **Shostakovich** after a novel by **Nikolai Leskov
*First performed in **Leningrad, 1934***
*Approximate length **150 minutes***

At first *Lady Macbeth* was a great success both in Russia and abroad, but it was condemned in 1936 by the official Russian Communist newspaper, *Pravda*. "Is its success abroad," *Pravda* asked, "not explained by the fact that it tickles the perverted bourgeois taste with its fidgety, screaming, neurotic music?" Katerina kills her father-in-law and then her husband for the sake of her servant and lover, Sergey. When their crimes are discovered, they are exiled to Siberia where Sergey seduces another convict. Katerina drowns her rival and then herself. The music, like the drama, has an atmosphere of intense foreboding.

JOHANN STRAUSS (1825–99)
DIE FLEDERMAUS (The Bat)

*Opera in **three acts** to a German libretto by **Carl Haffner**
and **Richard Genée** after **Meilhac** and **Halévy***
*First performed in **Vienna, 1874***
*Approximate length **135 minutes***

The most popular German comic opera, *Die Fledermaus*
combines all the liveliest elements of French comic opera
with warm Viennese musical charm. The support it has
received from great German conductors such as Karajan,
Kleiber and Krauss has ensured that, despite a quite ludi-
crous plot which involves an elaborate series of mistaken
identities, it has succeeded as the only operetta in the
regular repertory of the world's great opera houses. The
score is full of memorable numbers, not least Adele's
laughing song and the brilliant waltzing overture.

RICHARD STRAUSS (1864–1949)
SALOME

*Opera in **one act** to **Hedwig Lachmann's** German
translation of **Oscar Wilde's** eponymous play*
*First performed in **Dresden, 1905***
*Approximate length **105 minutes***

Like Oscar Wilde's original play, Strauss's *Salome* was
intended to shock. In fact the soprano Marie Wittich
refused to perform the famous "Dance of the seven veils"
at the premiere in 1905. "I won't do it," she
said, "I am a respectable married woman." To
tortured, ecstatic, often frenzied music, Salome
demands the head of John the Baptist with
which she enters a wild necrophiliac commu-
nion. Herod is so disgusted that he orders his
soldiers to crush her beneath their shields.

ELEKTRA

*Opera in **one act** to a German libretto by **Hugo
von Hofmannsthal** after **Sophocles'** tragedy*
*First performed in **Dresden, 1909***
*Approximate length **105 minutes***

A short but incredibly intense work that, like
Strauss's previous opera *Salome*, deals with the
feverish, psychotic behaviour of a young woman.

The swirling, surging sounds of Strauss's often very loud
music can be quite overwhelming. Elektra and her
brother, Orestes, avenge the murder of their father
Agamemnon by hacking their mother and her lover to
death with an axe. In a trance-like state, and overwhelmed
with excitement at the success of her actions, Elektra
swoons and dies during her victory dance.

DER ROSENKAVALIER (The Knight of the Rose)

*Opera in **three acts** to a German libretto by
Hugo von Hofmannsthal*
*First performed in **Dresden, 1911***
*Approximate length **195 minutes***

The combination of pain, sentiment and comedy with
rich orchestral scoring and a plethora of sentimental
Viennese melodies makes this one of the most sensual and
popular twentieth-century operas. Set in the aristocratic
salons of late eighteenth-century Vienna, the voluptuous
but middle-aged Marschallin is worried that her teenage
lover, Octavian (played by a female mezzo-soprano), will
eventually leave her for a younger woman. In the end he
finds happiness with beautiful Sophie von Faninal as the
Marschallin comes to terms with her loss.

Below Baron Ochs (third from right) disrupts the blossoming
affair between Sophie (second from right) and Octavian (far
right) in Act II of Richard Strauss's comedy, *Der Rosenkavalier.*

ARIADNE AUF NAXOS

Opera with a prelude and one act to a German
libretto by Hugo von Hofmannsthal
First performed in Stuttgart, 1912; revised version
Vienna, 1916
Approximate length 120 minutes

In one of Strauss's most beautiful and uplifting works, an opera company and a *commedia dell'arte* theatre troupe are asked by their rich patron to run their acts simultaneously so that both shows are over in time for a fireworks display. The synthesis of comic pantomime and tragic opera is brilliantly worked, while the music in the final scene ranks among Strauss's most ethereal. The opera follows in a tradition of moving soprano endings started by Wagner with his famous "Liebestod" (love-death) from *Tristan and Isolde*.

Above Kathleen Battle (Zerbinetta) and Olaf Baer (the harlequin) in *Ariadne auf Naxos* by Richard Strauss.

IGOR STRAVINSKY (1882–1971)
THE RAKE'S PROGRESS

Opera in three acts to an English libretto by W.H. Auden
and Chester Kallman after Hogarth's engravings
First performed in Venice, 1951
Approximate length 135 minutes

As the culminating masterpiece of Stravinsky's neoclassical period, *The Rake's Progress* recreates the graceful spirit of the Classical opera without losing an ounce of Stravinsky's individual musical voice in the process. Auden's brilliantly witty words are an essential ingredient in a plot that follows the moral descent of Tom Rakewell from a debauched multi-millionaire to a gibbering and bankrupted lunatic. His Mephistophelean servant Nick Shadow, his ex-fiancée Anne Truelove and his curious bearded wife, Baba the Turk, all contribute to the cruelty of this comedy.

ARTHUR SULLIVAN (1842–1900)
THE MIKADO

Opera in two acts to an English libretto by W.S. Gilbert
First performed in London, 1885
Approximate length 135 minutes

Sullivan had a great genius for melody and, like so many of his other comic operettas, *The Mikado* consists of one inspired tune after another. The story, a farce set in Japan, is hilariously constructed. Among the highlights of the work are "A wandering minstrel I" and "Tit Willow," while the overture is a medley of many of the operetta's finest tunes.

PYOTR ILYICH TCHAIKOVSKY (1840–93)
EUGENE ONEGIN

Opera in three acts to a Russian libretto by Tchaikovsky
and Konstantin Shilovsky after a poem by Pushkin
First performed in Moscow, 1879
Approximate length 150 minutes

A beautifully moody work in which the young Tatiana is spurned by the sophisticated Onegin to whom she has penned a long, frank declaration of love. Years later, when she is married to an old aristocrat, Prince Gremin, she meets Onegin at a St Petersburg ball. This time it is Onegin who declares his love for her, but while she loves him she will remain true to her husband. Highlights include the famously moving letter scene and a dramatic pistol duel between Onegin and his erstwhile friend, Lensky.

THE QUEEN OF SPADES

Opera in three acts to a Russian libretto by Tchaikovsky and
his brother, Modest Tchaikovsky, after the novella by
Aleksandr Pushkin
First performed in St Petersburg, 1890
Approximate length 160 minutes

For many years this was considered a weaker work than Tchaikovsky's most famous opera, *Eugene Onegin*, but

Above Leone Rysanek in Tchaikovsky's *Queen of Spades*, performed at the Metropolitan Opera House in New York.

fashions change and today *The Queen of Spades* is generally considered as fine a masterpiece as any Tchaikovsky composed. Hermann, an impoverished soldier, loves Lisa who is betrothed to a prince. This leads to Hermann's obsession with gambling; he frightens Lisa's grandmother to death trying to extract from her the secret to winning at cards, before driving Lisa to suicide and eventually losing all his money in a game with Lisa's fiancé. His own suicide is hastened by the ghost of the old lady. Tchaikovsky's music is every bit as obsessive as Pushkin's plot and, like *Onegin*, this opera contains many spectacular balletic scenes as well as an elegant Classical song borrowed from the French composer André Grétry (1741–1813).

CARL MARIA VON WEBER (1786–1826)
DER FREISCHUTZ (The Freeshooter)
Opera in three acts to a German libretto by Friedrich Kind
First performed in Berlin, 1821
Approximate length 150 minutes

Der Freischütz is a notable and early example of German Romantic opera. The theme of woodland magic (which recurs in Wagner's Ring, Humperdinck's *Hänsel und Gretel* and elsewhere) is presented here in the form of a huntsman's magic bullets. To win the hand of Agathe, Max must win a shooting competition, and to this end he enlists the help of the evil

spirit Samiel. Max's first six magic bullets hit the target, but his seventh is directed by Samiel to kill the evil huntsman, Kaspar. In the end Max is forgiven, and he and Agathe are eventually united.

KURT WEILL (1900–50)
DIE DREIGROSCHENOPER
(The Threepenny Opera)
Opera in three acts to a German libretto by Bertolt Brecht after The Beggar's Opera
First performed in Berlin, 1928
Approximate length 135 minutes

Based on John Gay's *Beggar's Opera*, conceived two hundred years earlier, Kurt Weill composed his numbers in a popular, jazz-inspired style to accompany a sleazy story of London low-life criminals. The most illuminating feature of this work are the tunes, many of which (most notably the "Ballad of Mack the Knife") have enjoyed popularity as separate songs in their own right. Strictly speaking it could be argued that the *Threepenny Opera* is not an opera – more a ballad-musical perhaps, though the libretto itself makes it more complex than a straight musical entertainment.

Below The gripping penultimate scene – the shooting competition – of Weber's magical opera, *Der Freischütz*, in a production staged at the Royal Opera House, London.

OPERA HOUSES AND FESTIVALS

An adventurous opera-goer could find an opera house or festival in almost every country in the world. Some of the most celebrated are listed below.

ARGENTINA

The famous Teatro Colón in **Buenos Aires**, inaugurated in 1908 and with a capacity for 4000 spectators, is the most important opera house in Latin America. It regularly plays host to the world's most prestigious singers, with standard as well as adventurous repertoire including many new works by Argentinian composers.

AUSTRALIA

Opened in 1973, the **Sydney** Opera House sits on a harbour promontory, providing the city with its most prominent architectural feature. The house is home to Australia's only full-time opera company and once provided a regular stage for Joan Sutherland, who performed most of her best roles here with her conductor husband, Richard Bonynge (Music Director 1975–86).

AUSTRIA

Vienna has long been an important operatic capital of the world. The opera house, bombed in World War II, was reopened in 1955. Today enjoying a vast public subsidy, Vienna State Opera produces some of the most lavish and thoroughly rehearsed performances in the world. The annual festival at **Salzburg** (Mozart's birthplace) in late July and August is undoubtedly Europe's premiere opera festival, attracting many of the world's most famous singers and conductors. A rich variety of opera and operetta is also offered at the summertime lakeside festival at **Bregenz** in Vorarlberg, west Austria.

FRANCE

Paris has a busy operatic calendar with full-scale works regularly performed at the Opéra Comique, the Théâtre des Champs-Elysées and the Théâtre du Châtelet, but the most important operatic venue is now the vast new Opéra Bastille, opened in 1990. Outside Paris, the Opéra de **Lyon** has a reputation for innovative programming and a high standard of performances. The main French opera festivals are at **Aix-en-Provence** and **Avignon** in July.

GERMANY

Many German towns boast an opera house, the most famous being at **Munich**, **Hamburg** and **Berlin**. The Mecca for Wagner fans is in the Bavarian town of **Bayreuth**, where the theatre was built to the specifications of the composer himself during the 1870s. It seats 1925 spectators. The festival, which performs only Wagner's works, has an uncomfortable wooden auditorium but the acoustics are extraordinarily good. The festival is so popular that tickets are never easy to obtain at late notice.

IRELAND

The small harbour town of **Wexford** is home to a festival specializing in rare nineteenth-century operas, often little-known works by famous composers. Standards are high, even without big-name stars, and the festival attracts many of the world's most enthusiastic opera-lovers.

ITALY

The grandest and most famous opera house in Italy is La Scala, only one of five opera houses in **Milan**. The present building dates from the 1790s but was largely rebuilt after bomb damage in 1943. Among the notable premieres to have taken place here are Verdi's *Otello* and *Falstaff* and Bellini's *Norma*. Today the repertoire is wide-ranging and the atmosphere exciting. Riccardo Muti was appointed Music Director in 1986, succeeding Claudio Abbado. There are important opera houses in many other Italian towns, notably **Rome**, **Naples**, **Bologna** and **Venice** (where the famous La Fenice was sadly destroyed by fire in 1996). Annual festivals celebrating the works of Rossini at **Pesaro** and Puccini at **Torre del Lago** have proved popular, as have the spectacular summer seasons at the famous outdoor arena in **Verona**.

RUSSIA

Funding has been difficult for the two leading Russian opera houses in recent years, as it has been for other Eastern European companies (such as Prague, Budapest, Brno). Even so, spectacular productions continue to be staged by the Kirov Opera in **St Petersburg**, under the inspired leadership of Music Director Valery Gergiev, and at the Bolshoi Opera in **Moscow**. Both companies excel at productions of Russian "grand opera."

SPAIN

For the keen operatic visitor, Spain's rich tradition of *zarzuela* (a unique form of national operetta) can be sampled at the Teatro Lirico Nacional de la Zarzuela in **Madrid**. Standard operatic repertoire outside of Madrid is regularly performed in **Barcelona**, **Seville**, **Bilbao** and **Cadiz**.

SWEDEN

Drottningholm Court Theatre, with a capacity of under 500, was built in 1766 at the Swedish Royal Palace on Lake Maleren just outside Stockholm. It is an exceptionally well-preserved theatre, with much of its original backstage machinery still in working order. The May to September festival concentrates on works of the Baroque and Classical eras. With a period-instrument orchestra in period costume, Drottningholm is quite unique.

UNITED KINGDOM

At **London**'s Royal Opera House, Covent Garden, operas are presented in a long season running from September to July. The resident company prides itself on lavish productions using a high level of international talent. All operas are presented in their original languages, with translated surtitles above the stage. Bernard Haitink has been Music Director

here since 1987. The opera house will be closed for reconstruction from July 1997 until 1999. English National Opera, also in London, offers cheaper seats at the Coliseum. All operas are sung in English. Productions are often stylish and modern. At a country house in **Glyndebourne**, Sussex, a world-class opera festival runs from late May to August every year. Opera lovers can picnic during the long interval in spectacular gardens. Other important venues in the UK include **Leeds** (Opera North), **Cardiff** (Welsh National Opera), **Glasgow** (Scottish Opera) and the **Edinburgh** Festival.

UNITED STATES OF AMERICA

The Metropolitan Opera House, America's foremost opera venue, opened in 1966 at the Lincoln Center, **New**

York, as a new home for the distinguished Metropolitan Opera Company founded in 1883. Every major operatic star of the last thirty years has sung here. Both repertoire and style are conservative, with operas generally performed only after they have established themselves elsewhere. An innovative system of providing text translations on monitors on the backs of seats was introduced in the mid-1990s. James Levine has been Music Director here since 1976. New York City Opera (also at the Lincoln Center) is an imaginative rival. Other important US opera companies are to be found in **Chicago**, **San Francisco** and **Santa Fe**. Glimmerglass, the "American Glyndebourne," provides a showcase for young talent at an annual summer festival in **Cooperstown**, **New York**.

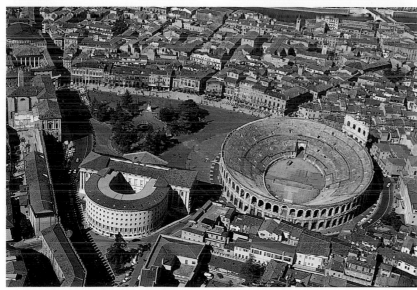

Top left The splendid Kirov Theatre in St Petersburg. *Top centre* The Royal Opera House in London. *Top right* The Metropolitan Opera House, New York, the premiere US opera venue. *Left* The spectacular arena in Verona (the second largest Roman arena in the world) plays host to lavish operatic productions in the summer. *Above* The famous landmark of the Sydney Opera House.

INDEX

1 **MASSENET**: "Nicias! Ah" from *Thaïs*, Act II, extract
(lib. Gallet after France)
Sherrill Milnes (Athanaël)
New Philharmonia Orchestra conducted by Lorin Maazel
℗ 1976 EMI Records Ltd.

2 **PUCCINI**: "Se la giurata" from *Tosca*, Act II, extract
(lib. Illica and Giacosa)
Tito Gobbi (Scarpia), Maria Callas (Tosca)
Orchestra of La Scala, Milan conducted by Victor De Sabata
℗ 1953 EMI Records Ltd.

3 **DONIZETTI**: Mad Scene from *Lucia di Lammermoor*,
Act III, extract (lib. Cammarano after Scott)
Maria Callas (Lucia)
Philharmonia Orchestra conducted by Tullio Serafin
℗ 1960 EMI Records Ltd.

4 **MOZART**: Overture from *Don Giovanni*, extract
Philharmonia Orchestra conducted by Carlo Maria Giulini
℗ 1961 EMI Records Ltd.

5 **WAGNER**: Overture from *Die Meistersinger von
Nürnberg*, extract
Bavarian State Orchestra conducted by Wolfgang Sawallisch
℗ 1994 EMI Records Ltd.

6 **MONTEVERDI**: Overture from *L'Orfeo*, extract
London Baroque, London Cornett and Sackbut Ensemble
directed by Charles Medlam
℗ 1984 EMI Records Ltd.

7 **VERDI**: Overture from *Aida*, extract
New Philharmonia Orchestra conducted by Riccardo Muti
℗ 1974 EMI Records Ltd.

8 **PUCCINI**: Overture from *La Bohème*, extract
Orchestra of the Opera House, Rome conducted by
Thomas Schippers
℗ 1964 EMI Records Ltd.

9 **HANDEL**: "Ah! Ruggiero crudel" from *Alcina*, Act II, extract
Arleen Augér (Alcina)
City of London Baroque Sinfonia conducted by Richard Hickox
℗ 1986 EMI Records Ltd.

10 **BEETHOVEN**: "Abscheulicher!" from *Fidelio*, Act I, extract
(lib. Sonnleithner and Treitschke)
Helga Dernesch (Leonore)
Berlin Philharmonic Orchestra conducted by Herbert
Von Karajan
℗ 1971 EMI Records Ltd.

11 **WAGNER**: "Was Macht dich" from *Lohengrin*, Act II, extract
Dunja Vejzovic (Ortrud)
Berlin Philharmonic Orchestra conducted by Herbert Von Karajan
℗ 1982 EMI Records Ltd.

12a **WAGNER**: "Schläfst du" from *Götterdämmerung*,
Act II, extract
Theo Adam (Alberich)
Bavarian Radio Symphony Orchestra conducted by
Bernard Haitink
℗ 1992 EMI Records Ltd.

12b **WAGNER**: "Sleep you" from *Götterdämmerung*,
Act II, extract
Derek Hammound Stroud (Alberich)
English National Opera Orchestra conducted by
Reginald Goodall
℗ 1978 EMI Records Ltd.

13a **VERDI**: "Celeste Aida" from *Aida*, Act I, extract
(lib. Ghislanzoni)
Franco Corelli (Radamès)
Orchestra of the Opera House, Rome conducted by
Zubin Mehta
℗ 1967 EMI Records Ltd.

13b **VERDI**: "Celeste Aida" from *Aida*, Act I, extract (lib.
Ghislanzoni)
Placido Domingo (Radamès)
New Philharmonia Orchestra conducted by Riccardo Muti
℗ 1974 EMI Records Ltd.

14a **VERDI**: "O patria mia" from *Aida*, Act III, extract
(lib. Ghislanzoni)
Birgit Nilsson (Aida)
Orchestra of the Opera House, Rome conducted by
Zubin Mehta
℗ 1967 EMI Records Ltd.

14b **VERDI**: "O patria mia" from *Aida*, Act III, extract
(lib. Ghislanzoni)
Montserrat Caballé (Aida)
New Philharmonia Orchestra conducted by Riccardo Muti
℗ 1974 EMI Records Ltd.

15 **MOZART**: "Der Hölle Rache" from *Die Zauberflöte*, Act II,
extract (lib. Schikaneder)
Edita Gruberová (Queen of the Night)
Bavarian Radio Symphony Orchestra conducted by
Bernard Haitink
℗ 1981 EMI Records Ltd.

16 **VERDI**: "L'abborita rivale" from *Aida*, Act IV, extract
(lib. Ghislanzoni)
Fiorenza Cossotto (Amneris)
New Philharmonia Orchestra conducted by Riccardo Muti
℗ 1974 EMI Records Ltd.

17 **SULLIVAN**: "Alone and yet alive" from *The Mikado*, Act II,
extract (lib. Gilbert)
Monica Sinclair (Katisha)
Pro Arte Orchestra conducted by Sir Malcolm Sargent
℗ 1957 EMI Records Ltd.

18 **HANDEL**: "Ombra mai fu" from *Serse*, Act I, extract (lib.
Minato and Stampiglia)
Gérard Lesne
Il Seminario Musicale
℗ 1995 EMI France

19 **WAGNER**: "Wie sie selig" from *Tristan und Isolde*, Act III
Jon Vickers (Tristan)
Berlin Philharmonic Orchestra conducted by Herbert Von Karajan
℗ 1972 EMI Records Ltd.

20 **MOZART**: "Non più andrai" from *Le nozze di Figaro*, Act I, extract (lib. Da Ponte)
Giuseppe Taddei (Figaro)
Philharmonia Orchestra conducted by Carlo Maria Giulini
℗ 1961 EMI Records Ltd.

21 **DONIZETTI**: "Ah! Un foco insolito" from *Don Pasquale*, Act I, extract (lib. Donizetti and Ruffini)
Sesto Bruscantini (Don Pasquale)
Philharmonia Orchestra conducted by Riccardo Muti
℗ 1984 EMI Records Ltd.

22 **VERDI**: "Il santo nome" from *La forza del destino*, Act II, extract (lib. Piave)
Paul Plishka (Padre Guardiano)
Orchestra of La Scala, Milan conducted by Riccardo Muti
℗ 1986 EMI Records Ltd.

23 **VERDI**: "Va pensiero" from *Nabucco*, Act III, extract (lib. Solera)
Ambrosian Opera Chorus
(Chorus Master: John McCarthy)
Philharmonia Orchestra conducted by Riccardo Muti
℗ 1978 EMI Records Ltd.

24 **MONTEVERDI**: "Vi ricorda" from *L'Orfeo*, Act II, extract (lib. Striggio)
Nigel Rogers (Orfeo)
London Baroque directed by Charles Medlam
℗ 1984 EMI Records Ltd.

25 **GLUCK**: "Che farò senza Euridice?" from *Orfeo ed Euridice*, Act III, extract (lib. Calzabigi)
Agnes Baltsa (Orfeo)
Philharmonia Orchestra conducted by Riccardo Muti
℗ 1982 EMI Records Ltd.

26 **BELLINI**: "Casta diva" from *Norma*, Act I, extract (lib. Romani)
Jane Eaglen (Norma)
Orchestra of the Maggio Musicale Fiorentino conducted by Riccardo Muti
℗ 1995 EMI Records Ltd.

27 **PUCCINI**: "Quando me'n vo' soletta" from *La Bohème*, Act II, extract (lib. Illica and Giacosa)
Mariella Adani (Musetta)
Orchestra of the Opera House, Rome conducted by Thomas Schippers
℗ 1964 EMI Records Ltd.

28 **PURCELL**: "When I am laid in earth" from *Dido and Aeneas*, Act III (lib. Tate)
Victoria de los Angeles (Dido)
English Chamber Orchestra conducted by Sir John Barbirolli
℗ 1966 EMI Records Ltd.

29 **PURCELL**: Overture from *Dido and Aeneas*, Act I
English Chamber Orchestra conducted by Sir John Barbirolli
℗ 1966 EMI Records Ltd.

30 **MOZART**: "Là ci darem la mano" from *Don Giovanni*, Act I (lib. Da Ponte)
Graziella Sciutti (Zerlina), Eberhard Wächter (Don Giovanni)
Philharmonia Orchestra conducted by Carlo Maria Giulini
℗ 1961 EMI Records Ltd.

31 **MOZART**: "Madamina il catalogo" from *Don Giovanni*, Act I, extract (lib. Da Ponte)
Giuseppe Taddei (Leporello)
Philharmonia Orchestra conducted by Carlo Maria Giulini
℗ 1961 EMI Records Ltd.

32 **ROSSINI**: "Largo al factotum" from *Il barbiere di Siviglia*, Act I (lib. Sterbini)
Tito Gobbi (Figaro)
Philharmonia Orchestra conducted by Alceo Galliera
℗ 1958 EMI Records Ltd.

33 **ROSSINI**: Overture from *Il barbiere di Siviglia*, extract
Philharmonia Orchestra conducted by Alceo Galliera
℗ 1958 EMI Records Ltd.

34 **VERDI**: "Bella figlia dell'amore" from *Rigoletto*, Act III (lib. Piave)
Vincenzo La Scola (Duke), Martha Senn (Maddalena), Daniella Dessì (Gilda), Giorgio Zancanaro (Rigoletto)
Orchestra of La Scala, Milan conducted by Riccardo Muti
℗ 1988 EMI Records Ltd.

35 **VERDI**: "La donna è mobile" from *Rigoletto*, Act III (lib. Piave)
Vincenzo La Scola (Duke)
Orchestra of La Scala, Milan conducted by Riccardo Muti
℗ 1988 EMI Records Ltd.

36 **WAGNER**: "Morgenlich leuchtend" from *Die Meistersinger von Nurnberg*, Act III
Ben Heppner (Walther)
Bavarian State Orchestra conducted by Wolfgang Sawallisch
℗ 1994 EMI Records Ltd.

37 **WAGNER**: Riot scene from *Die Meistersinger von Nurnberg*, Act II, extract
Bavarian State Orchestra conducted by Wolfgang Sawallisch
℗ 1994 EMI Records Ltd.

38 **MUSSORGSKY**: Coronation scene from *Boris Godunov*, Act I
Polish Radio Chorus of Krakow
Polish Radio National Symphony Orchestra conducted by Jerzy Semkow
℗ 1977 EMI Records Ltd.

39 **MUSSORGSKY**: Finale from *Boris Godunov*, Act IV, extract
Paulos Raptis (Simpleton)
Polish Radio National Symphony Orchestra conducted by Jerzy Semkow
℗ 1977 EMI Records Ltd.

40 **BIZET**: "L'amour est un oiseau rebelle" (Habanera) from *Carmen*, Act I (lib. Meilhac and Halévy)
Victoria de los Angeles (Carmen)
French Radio National Orchestra conducted by Sir Thomas Beecham, Bart., C.H.
℗ 1960 EMI France

41 **BIZET**: Death Scene from *Carmen*, Act IV, extract (lib. Meilhac and Halévy)
Victoria De Los Angeles (Carmen), Nicolai Gedda (Don José)
French Radio National Orchestra conducted by Sir Thomas Beecham, Bart., C.H.
℗ 1960 EMI France

42 **PUCCINI**: "Vissi d'arte" from *Tosca*, Act II (lib. Illica and Giacosa)
Maria Callas (Tosca)
Orchestra of La Scala, Milan conducted by Victor De Sabata
℗ 1953 EMI Records Ltd.

43 **PUCCINI**: "Recondita armonia" from *Tosca*, Act I, extract (lib. Illica and Giacosa)
Giuseppe di Stefano (Cavaradossi), Maria Callas (Tosca)
Orchestra of La Scala, Milan conducted by Victor de Sabata
℗ 1953 EMI Records Ltd.

ACKNOWLEDGMENTS

Abbreviations
b = below; c = centre; l = left; r = right; t = top

Jacket l PAL/Clive Barda **jacket bkgd, endpapers** AKG London **jacket back flap** Dan Stevens **3t** PAL/Clive Barda **4** Theatre Museum, V&A/Houston Rogers **8** PAL/Clive Barda **10t, c** PAL/Clive Barda **11** Archivio Ente Lirico Arena di Verona/Gianfranco Fainello **12** Photostage/©Donald Cooper **13 bkgd** AKG London **13c** PAL/Clive Barda **13cr** PAL/Emily Booth **14l** PAL/Ron Scherl **14r** Photostage/©Donald Cooper **15** Henry Grossman **16** Photostage/©Donald Cooper **17cl, cr, b** Vivianne Purdom **18t** AKG London **18c** Archivio Ente Lirico Arena di Verona/Gianfranco Fainello **19t** PAL/Ron Scherl **19b** Foto Fayer **20c** Archivio Ente Lirico Arena di Verona/ Gianfranco Fainello **22cl** Photostage/©Donald Cooper **22cr** PAL/Clive Barda **22bl** Henry Grossman **22br** PAL/Gianfranco Fainello **23bkgd** AKG London **24** Photostage/©Donald Cooper **25t** Archivio Ente Lirico Arena di Verona/Gianfranco Fainello **25b** Zoë Dominic **26tr** Photostage/©Donald Cooper **26cl** Lebrecht Collection **26bl** Metropolitan Opera/Winnie Klotz **26br** Photostage/©Donald Cooper **27tr** Zoë Dominic **27cr** Catherine Ashmore **28t** PAL/Clive Barda **28c** Catherine Ashmore **29t, c, b** PAL/Clive Barda **30–39** Sue Adler **40** Giancarlo Costa/Museo Bibliografico Musicale, Bologna **42, 43t** Jean-Loup Charmet/Bibliothèque de l'Opéra, Paris **43c** AKG London/National Gallery **43b** Reg Wilson **44t** Henry Grossman **44b** Theatre Museum,V&A/Houston Rogers **45t** Hulton Deustch/Baron **45c** Lebrecht Collection **46, 47t** Giancarlo Costa **47b** Archivio IGDA/Museo Conservatorio, Bologna **48t** PAL/Ron Scherl **48c** Catherine Ashmore **49t** Giancarlo Costa **49b** Natalia Gontcharova: design for *The Golden Cockerel*, 1914. AKG London/Erich Lessing/AA Bakhruschion Museum, Moscow/ ©ADAGP, Paris and DACS, London 1996 **50c** AKG London **50b** Giancarlo Costa **51t** PAL/Clive Barda **51b** PAL/Fritz Curzon **52** Lebrecht Collection/André Le Coz **55bkgd** AKG London **56** Operan/Mats Bäcker **57** Archivio IGDA/Glynde- bourne Festival Opera **58** Malcolm Keep **59** AKG London/ National Gallery **60t** AKG London/Paul Mellon Collection, USA **60b** Reg Wilson **61** Photostage/©Donald Cooper **62** AKG London/Theatermuseum, Munich **63** Photostage/©Donald Cooper **64l** AKG London **64r** Australian Opera **65** Lebrecht Collection **66** Gaumont/Camera One/OFP/Janus (courtesy Kobal) **67** AKG London/Mozarteum, Salzburg **68t** Reg Wilson **68b** Metropolitan Opera/Winnie Klotz **69** Photostage/©Donald Cooper **70** Theatre Museum, V&A/Houston Rogers **71** Giancarlo Costa **72** Myles Birket Foster: *Seville*. Bridgeman Art Library/Townley Hall Art Gallery & Museum, Burnley **73** Reg Wilson **74** Giancarlo Costa **75, 76** Reg Wilson **77l, r, 78** Photostage/©Donald Cooper **79** AKG London **80** Lebrecht Collection **81** G Ricordi & Co **82** AKG London **83, 84t** Giancarlo Costa **84b** Teatro alla Scala/Lelli & Masotti **85** Metropolitan Opera/Winnie Klotz **86** Reg Wilson **88** Royal Opera House Archives **89** Hans Wurm: *Panorama of Nuremburg, c.1510–20*. AKG London/Germanisches National-museum, Nürnberg **90** Royal Opera House Archives **91** AKG London **92** Metropolitan Opera/Winnie Klotz **93** AKG London/Franz Hanfstaengl **94** Metropolitan Opera/Winnie Klotz **95c, b** Photostage/©Donald Cooper **96** ET Archive/Historical Museum, Moscow **97** Theatre Museum, V&A/Houston Rogers **98** Archivio IGDA **99** Edward Gaertner: *Moscow, 1839*. Archivio IGDA **100** Lebrecht Collection **101** Royal Opera House Archives **102** Catherine Ashmore **103t** Fedorowsky: costume designs for *Khovanschina*. Giancarlo Costa **103b** Photostage/ ©Donald Cooper **104** Opera/Gaumont (courtesy Kobal) **105** Archivio IGDA/Bibliothèque de l'Opéra, Paris/©Lila de Nobili **106** Photostage/©Donald Cooper **107** Theatre Museum, V&A/ Houston Rogers **108** Archivio IGDA/Bibliothèque de l'Opéra, Paris **109** Giancarlo Costa **110t** AKG London/Nadar **110b** Giancarlo Costa **111l** Photostage/©Donald Cooper **111r** Sarasota Opera/Stephen LeBlanc **112** Rada Film srl, Rome **113** Theatre Museum, V&A/Houston Rogers **114** Australian Opera **115** Theatre Museum, V&A/Houston Rogers **116** Archivio IGDA/Villa Puccini, Torre del Lago **117** Lebrecht Collection **118** Photostage/©Donald Cooper **119t** Metropolitan Opera/Winnie Klotz **119b** Archivio Ente Lirico Arena di Verona/Gianfranco Fainello **120tl** Carol Rosegg **120tc, tr, b** PAL/Clive Barda **120cr** Henry Grossman **122l** Carol Rosegg **122r** Reg Wilson **123** Photostage/©Donald Cooper **124** Henry Grossman **125l** AKG London **125r, 126, 127t** PAL/Clive Barda **127b, 128l** Henry Grossman **128r** Catherine Ashmore **129** Carol Rosegg **130c** PAL/Ron Scherl **130b** PAL/Clive Barda **131l** Chatelet Theatre Musical de Paris/©Marie-Noëlle Robert **131r** Catherine Ashmore **132l** PAL/Ron Scherl **132r** Bayerische Staatsoper/©Wilfred Hösl **133** Photostage/©Donald Cooper **134** Reg Wilson **135t** Henry Grossman **135b** Reg Wilson **137cl** Catherine Ashmore **137c** PAL/Clive Barda **137cr** Robert Harding Picture Library **137bl** Archivio Ente Lirico Arena di Verona/Gianfranco Fainello **137br** Julia Ruxton

While every effort has been made to trace the present copyright holders we apologize in advance for any unintentional omission or error and will be pleased to insert the appropriate acknowledg- ment in any subsequent edition.

The publishers would like to thank Jane Livingston, Henry Little and Laurence Holderness at English National Opera for all their help and cooperation; Duncan Moore and Keith Hilton at EMI for their invaluable advice; and Juliet Bending for compiling the index.